Civil Jurisdiction and Judgments Act 1982

CHAPTER 27

ARRANGEMENT OF SECTIONS

PART I

IMPLEMENTATION OF THE CONVENTIONS

Main implementing provisions

PART II

JURISDICTION, AND RECOGNITION AND ENFORCEMENT OF JUDGMENTS, WITHIN UNITED KINGDOM

PART III

JURISDICTION IN SCOTLAND

PART IV

MISCELLANEOUS PROVISIONS

Provisions relating to jurisdiction

Provisions relating to recognition and enforcement of judgments

ELIZABETH II

Civil Jurisdiction and Judgments Act 1982

1982 CHAPTER 27

An Act to make further provision about the jurisdiction of courts and tribunals in the United Kingdom and certain other territories and about the recognition and enforcement of judgments given in the United Kingdom or elsewhere; to provide for the modification of certain provisions relating to legal aid; and for connected purposes. [13th July 1982]

BE IT ENACTED by the Queen's most Excellent Majesty, by and with the advice and consent of the Lords Spiritual and Temporal, and Commons, in this present Parliament assembled, and by the authority of the same, as follows:—

PART I

IMPLEMENTATION OF THE CONVENTIONS

Main implementing provisions

Interpretation of references to the Conventions and Contracting States.

1.—(1) In this Act—

" the 1968 Convention " means the Convention on jurisdiction and the enforcement of judgments in civil and commercial matters (including the Protocol annexed to that Convention), signed at Brussels on 27th September 1968;

" the 1971 Protocol " means the Protocol on the interpretation of the 1968 Convention by the European Court, signed at Luxembourg on 3rd June 1971;

PART I

" the Accession Convention " means the Convention on the accession to the 1968 Convention and the 1971 Protocol of Denmark, the Republic of Ireland and the United Kingdom, signed at Luxembourg on 9th October 1978 ;

" the Conventions " means the 1968 Convention, the 1971 Protocol and the Accession Convention.

(2) In this Act, unless the context otherwise requires—

(*a*) references to, or to any provision of, the 1968 Convention or the 1971 Protocol are references to that Convention, Protocol or provision as amended by the Accession Convention ; and

(*b*) any reference to a numbered Article is a reference to the Article so numbered of the 1968 Convention, and any reference to a sub-division of a numbered Article shall be construed accordingly.

(3) In this Act " Contracting State " means—

(*a*) one of the original parties to the 1968 Convention (Belgium, the Federal Republic of Germany, France, Italy, Luxembourg and the Netherlands) ; or

(*b*) one of the parties acceding to that Convention under the Accession Convention (Denmark, the Republic of Ireland and the United Kingdom),

being a state in respect of which the Accession Convention has entered into force in accordance with Article 39 of that Convention.

The Conventions to have the force of law.

2.—(1) The Conventions shall have the force of law in the United Kingdom, and judicial notice shall be taken of them.

(2) For convenience of reference there are set out in Schedules 1, 2 and 3 respectively the English texts of—

(*a*) the 1968 Convention as amended by Titles II and III of the Accession Convention ;

(*b*) the 1971 Protocol as amended by Title IV of the Accession Convention ; and

(*c*) Titles V and VI of the Accession Convention (transitional and final provisions),

being texts prepared from the authentic English texts referred to in Articles 37 and 41 of the Accession Convention.

Interpretation of the Conventions.

3.—(1) Any question as to the meaning or effect of any provision of the Conventions shall, if not referred to the European Court in accordance with the 1971 Protocol, be determined in accordance with the principles laid down by and any relevant decision of the European Court.

(2) Judicial notice shall be taken of any decision of, or expression of opinion by, the European Court on any such question.

(3) Without prejudice to the generality of subsection (1), the following reports (which are reproduced in the Official Journal of the Communities), namely—

(*a*) the reports by Mr. P. Jenard on the 1968 Convention and the 1971 Protocol; and O.J. 1979 No. C59/1 and 66.

(*b*) the report by Professor Peter Schlosser on the Accession Convention, O.J. 1979 No. C59/71.

may be considered in ascertaining the meaning or effect of any provision of the Conventions and shall be given such weight as is appropriate in the circumstances.

Supplementary provisions as to recognition and enforcement of judgments

Enforcement of judgments other than maintenance orders.

4.—(1) A judgment, other than a maintenance order, which is the subject of an application under Article 31 for its enforcement in any part of the United Kingdom shall, to the extent that its enforcement is authorised by the appropriate court, be registered in the prescribed manner in that court.

In this subsection " the appropriate court " means the court to which the application is made in pursuance of Article 32 (that is to say, the High Court or the Court of Session).

(2) Where a judgment is registered under this section, the reasonable costs or expenses of and incidental to its registration shall be recoverable as if they were sums recoverable under the judgment.

(3) A judgment registered under this section shall, for the purposes of its enforcement, be of the same force and effect, the registering court shall have in relation to its enforcement the same powers, and proceedings for or with respect to its enforcement may be taken, as if the judgment had been originally given by the registering court and had (where relevant) been entered.

(4) Subsection (3) is subject to Article 39 (restriction on enforcement where appeal pending or time for appeal unexpired), to section 7 and to any provision made by rules of court as to the manner in which and conditions subject to which a judgment registered under this section may be enforced.

Recognition and enforcement of maintenance orders.

5.—(1) The function of transmitting to the appropriate court an application under Article 31 for the recognition or enforcement in the United Kingdom of a maintenance order shall be discharged—

(*a*) as respects England and Wales and Scotland, by the Secretary of State;

(*b*) as respects Northern Ireland, by the Lord Chancellor.

PART I

In this subsection "the appropriate court" means the magistrates' court or sheriff court having jurisdiction in the matter in accordance with the second paragraph of Article 32.

(2) Such an application shall be determined in the first instance by the prescribed officer of that court.

(3) Where on such an application the enforcement of the order is authorised to any extent, the order shall to that extent be registered in the prescribed manner in that court.

(4) A maintenance order registered under this section shall, for the purposes of its enforcement, be of the same force and effect, the registering court shall have in relation to its enforcement the same powers, and proceedings for or with respect to its enforcement may be taken, as if the order had been originally made by the registering court.

(5) Subsection (4) is subject to Article 39 (restriction on enforcement where appeal pending or time for appeal unexpired), to section 7 and to any provision made by rules of court as to the manner in which and conditions subject to which an order registered under this section may be enforced.

(6) A maintenance order which by virtue of this section is enforceable by a magistrates' court in England and Wales or Northern Ireland shall be enforceable in the same manner as an affiliation order made by that court.

(7) The payer under a maintenance order registered under this section in a magistrates' court in England and Wales or Northern Ireland shall give notice of any change of address to the clerk of that court.

A person who without reasonable excuse fails to comply with this subsection shall be guilty of an offence and liable on summary conviction to a fine not exceeding £50.

Appeals under Article 37, second paragraph and Article 41.

6.—(1) The single further appeal on a point of law referred to in Article 37, second paragraph and Article 41 in relation to the recognition or enforcement of a judgment other than a maintenance order lies—

(*a*) in England and Wales or Northern Ireland, to the Court of Appeal or to the House of Lords in accordance with Part II of the Administration of Justice Act 1969 (appeals direct from the High Court to the House of Lords); (1969 c. 58.)

(*b*) in Scotland, to the Inner House of the Court of Session.

(2) Paragraph (*a*) of subsection (1) has effect notwithstanding section 15(2) of the Administration of Justice Act 1969 (exclusion of direct appeal to the House of Lords in cases where no appeal to that House lies from a decision of the Court of Appeal).

PART I

(3) The single further appeal on a point of law referred to in Article 37, second paragraph and Article 41 in relation to the recognition or enforcement of a maintenance order lies—

(*a*) in England and Wales, to the High Court by way of case stated in accordance with section 111 of the Magistrates' Courts Act 1980; 1980 c. 43.

(*b*) in Scotland, to the Inner House of the Court of Session;

(*c*) in Northern Ireland, to the Court of Appeal.

Interest on registered judgments.

7.—(1) Subject to subsection (4), where in connection with an application for registration of a judgment under section 4 or 5 the applicant shows—

(*a*) that the judgment provides for the payment of a sum of money; and

(*b*) that in accordance with the law of the Contracting State in which the judgment was given interest on that sum is recoverable under the judgment from a particular date or time,

the rate of interest and the date or time from which it is so recoverable shall be registered with the judgment and, subject to any provision made under subsection (2), the debt resulting, apart from section 4(2), from the registration of the judgment shall carry interest in accordance with the registered particulars.

(2) Provision may be made by rules of court as to the manner in which and the periods by reference to which any interest payable by virtue of subsection (1) is to be calculated and paid, including provision for such interest to cease to accrue as from a prescribed date.

(3) Costs or expenses recoverable by virtue of section 4(2) shall carry interest as if they were the subject of an order for the payment of costs or expenses made by the registering court on the date of registration.

(4) Interest on arrears of sums payable under a maintenance order registered under section 5 in a magistrates' court in England and Wales or Northern Ireland shall not be recoverable in that court, but without prejudice to the operation in relation to any such order of section 2A of the Maintenance Orders Act 1958 or section 11A of the Maintenance and Affiliation Orders Act (Northern Ireland) 1966 (which enable interest to be recovered if the order is re-registered for enforcement in the High Court). 1958 c. 39. 1966 c. 35. (N.I.)

(5) Except as mentioned in subsection (4), debts under judgments registered under section 4 or 5 shall carry interest only as provided by this section.

PART I

Currency of payment under registered maintenance orders.

8.—(1) Sums payable in the United Kingdom under a maintenance order by virtue of its registration under section 5, including any arrears so payable, shall be paid in the currency of the United Kingdom.

(2) Where the order is expressed in any other currency, the amounts shall be converted on the basis of the exchange rate prevailing on the date of registration of the order.

(3) For the purposes of this section, a written certificate purporting to be signed by an officer of any bank in the United Kingdom and stating the exchange rate prevailing on a specified date shall be evidence, and in Scotland sufficient evidence, of the facts stated.

Other supplementary provisions

Provisions supplementary to Title VII of 1968 Convention.

9.—(1) The provisions of Title VII of the 1968 Convention (relationship between that convention and other conventions to which Contracting States are or may become parties) shall have effect in relation to—

(*a*) any statutory provision, whenever passed or made, implementing any such other convention in the United Kingdom ; and

(*b*) any rule of law so far as it has the effect of so implementing any such other convention,

as they have effect in relation to that other convention itself.

(2) Her Majesty may by Order in Council declare a provision of a convention entered into by the United Kingdom to be a provision whereby the United Kingdom assumed an obligation of a kind provided for in Article 59 (which allows a Contracting State to agree with a third State to withhold recognition in certain cases from a judgment given by a court in another Contracting State which took jurisdiction on one of the grounds mentioned in the second paragraph of Article 3).

Allocation within U.K. of jurisdiction with respect to trusts and consumer contracts.

10.—(1) The provisions of this section have effect for the purpose of allocating within the United Kingdom jurisdiction in certain proceedings in respect of which the 1968 Convention confers jurisdiction on the courts of the United Kingdom generally and to which section 16 does not apply.

(2) Any proceedings which by virtue of Article 5(6) (trusts) are brought in the United Kingdom shall be brought in the courts of the part of the United Kingdom in which the trust is domiciled.

PART I

(3) Any proceedings which by virtue of the first paragraph of Article 14 (consumer contracts) are brought in the United Kingdom by a consumer on the ground that he is himself domiciled there shall be brought in the courts of the part of the United Kingdom in which he is domiciled.

Proof and admissibility of certain judgments and related documents.

11.—(1) For the purposes of the 1968 Convention—

(*a*) a document, duly authenticated, which purports to be a copy of a judgment given by a court of a Contracting State other than the United Kingdom shall without further proof be deemed to be a true copy, unless the contrary is shown; and

(*b*) the original or a copy of any such document as is mentioned in Article 46(2) or 47 (supporting documents to be produced by a party seeking recognition or enforcement of a judgment) shall be evidence, and in Scotland sufficient evidence, of any matter to which it relates.

(2) A document purporting to be a copy of a judgment given by any such court as is mentioned in subsection (1)(*a*) is duly authenticated for the purposes of this section if it purports—

(*a*) to bear the seal of that court; or

(*b*) to be certified by any person in his capacity as a judge or officer of that court to be a true copy of a judgment given by that court.

(3) Nothing in this section shall prejudice the admission in evidence of any document which is admissible apart from this section.

Provision for issue of copies of, and certificates in connection with, U.K. judgments.

12. Rules of court may make provision for enabling any interested party wishing to secure under the 1968 Convention the recognition or enforcement in another Contracting State of a judgment given by a court in the United Kingdom to obtain, subject to any conditions specified in the rules—

(*a*) a copy of the judgment; and

(*b*) a certificate giving particulars relating to the judgment and the proceedings in which it was given.

Modifications to cover authentic instruments and court settlements.

13.—(1) Her Majesty may by Order in Council provide that—

(*a*) any provision of this Act relating to the recognition or enforcement in the United Kingdom or elsewhere of judgments to which the 1968 Convention applies; and

(*b*) any other statutory provision, whenever passed or made, so relating,

PART I

shall apply, with such modifications as may be specified in the Order, in relation to documents and settlements within Title IV of the 1968 Convention (authentic instruments and court settlements enforceable in the same manner as judgments) as if they were judgments to which that Convention applies.

(2) An Order in Council under this section may make different provision in relation to different descriptions of documents and settlements.

(3) Any Order in Council under this section shall be subject to annulment in pursuance of a resolution of either House of Parliament.

Modifications consequential on revision of the Conventions.

14.—(1) If at any time it appears to Her Majesty in Council that Her Majesty's Government in the United Kingdom have agreed to a revision of any of the Conventions, including in particular any revision connected with the accession to the 1968 Convention of one or more further states, Her Majesty may by Order in Council make such modifications of this Act or any other statutory provision, whenever passed or made, as Her Majesty considers appropriate in consequence of the revision.

(2) An Order in Council under this section shall not be made unless a draft of the Order has been laid before Parliament and approved by a resolution of each House of Parliament.

(3) In this section " revision " means an omission from, addition to or alteration of any of the Conventions and includes replacement of any of the Conventions to any extent by another convention, protocol or other description of international agreement.

Interpretation of Part I and consequential amendments.

15.—(1) In this Part, unless the context otherwise requires—

" judgment " has the meaning given by Article 25 ;

" maintenance order " means a maintenance judgment within the meaning of the 1968 Convention ;

" payer ", in relation to a maintenance order, means the person liable to make the payments for which the order provides ;

" prescribed " means prescribed by rules of court.

(2) References in this Part to a judgment registered under section 4 or 5 include, to the extent of its registration, references to a judgment so registered to a limited extent only.

(3) Anything authorised or required by the 1968 Convention or this Part to be done by, to or before a particular magistrates' court may be done by, to or before any magistrates' court acting for the same petty sessions area (or, in Northern Ireland, petty sessions district) as that court.

(4) The enactments specified in Part I of Schedule 12 shall have effect with the amendments specified there, being amendments consequential on this Part. PART I

PART II

JURISDICTION, AND RECOGNITION AND ENFORCEMENT OF JUDGMENTS, WITHIN UNITED KINGDOM

Allocation within U.K. of jurisdiction in certain civil proceedings.

16.—(1) The provisions set out in Schedule 4 (which contains a modified version of Title II of the 1968 Convention) shall have effect for determining, for each part of the United Kingdom, whether the courts of law of that part, or any particular court of law in that part, have or has jurisdiction in proceedings where—

(*a*) the subject-matter of the proceedings is within the scope of the 1968 Convention as determined by Article 1 (whether or not the Convention has effect in relation to the proceedings) ; and

(*b*) the defendant or defender is domiciled in the United Kingdom or the proceedings are of a kind mentioned in Article 16 (exclusive jurisdiction regardless of domicile).

(2) In Schedule 4 modifications of Title II of the 1968 Convention are indicated as follows—

(*a*) modifications by way of omission are indicated by dots ; and

(*b*) within each Article words resulting from modifications by way of addition or substitution are printed in heavy type.

(3) In determining any question as to the meaning or effect of any provision contained in Schedule 4—

(*a*) regard shall be had to any relevant principles laid down by the European Court in connection with Title II of the 1968 Convention and to any relevant decision of that court as to the meaning or effect of any provision of that Title ; and

(*b*) without prejudice to the generality of paragraph (*a*), the reports mentioned in section 3(3) may be considered and shall, so far as relevant, be given such weight as is appropriate in the circumstances.

(4) The provisions of this section and Schedule 4 shall have effect subject to the 1968 Convention and to the provisions of section 17.

PART II

1950 c. 37.

(5) In section 15(1)(*a*) of the Maintenance Orders Act 1950 (domestic proceedings in which initial process may be served in another part of the United Kingdom), after sub-paragraph (v) there shall be added—

" (vi) Article 5(2) of Schedule 4 to the Civil Jurisdiction and Judgments Act 1982 ; or ".

Exclusion of certain proceedings from Schedule 4.

17.—(1) Schedule 4 shall not apply to proceedings of any description listed in Schedule 5 or to proceedings in Scotland under any enactment which confers jurisdiction on a Scottish court in respect of a specific subject-matter on specific grounds.

(2) Her Majesty may by Order in Council—

(*a*) add to the list in Schedule 5 any description of proceedings in any part of the United Kingdom ; and

(*b*) remove from that list any description of proceedings in any part of the United Kingdom (whether included in the list as originally enacted or added by virtue of this subsection).

(3) An Order in Council under subsection (2)—

(*a*) may make different provisions for different descriptions of proceedings, for the same description of proceedings in different courts or for different parts of the United Kingdom ; and

(*b*) may contain such transitional and other incidental provisions as appear to Her Majesty to be appropriate.

(4) An Order in Council under subsection (2) shall not be made unless a draft of the Order has been laid before Parliament and approved by a resolution of each House of Parliament.

Enforcement of U.K. judgments in other parts of U.K.

18.—(1) In relation to any judgment to which this section applies—

(*a*) Schedule 6 shall have effect for the purpose of enabling any money provisions contained in the judgment to be enforced in a part of the United Kingdom other than the part in which the judgment was given ; and

(*b*) Schedule 7 shall have effect for the purpose of enabling any non-money provisions so contained to be so enforced.

(2) In this section " judgment " means any of the following (references to the giving of a judgment being construed accordingly)—

(*a*) any judgment or order (by whatever name called) given or made by a court of law in the United Kingdom ;

(*b*) any judgment or order not within paragraph (*a*) which has been entered in England and Wales or Northern Ireland in the High Court or a county court ; PART II

(*c*) any document which in Scotland has been registered for execution in the Books of Council and Session or in the sheriff court books kept for any sheriffdom ;

(*d*) any award or order made by a tribunal in any part of the United Kingdom which is enforceable in that part without an order of a court of law ;

(*e*) an arbitration award which has become enforceable in the part of the United Kingdom in which it was given in the same manner as a judgment given by a court of law in that part ;

and, subject to the following provisions of this section, this section applies to all such judgments.

(3) Subject to subsection (4), this section does not apply to—

(*a*) a judgment given in proceedings in a magistrates' court in England and Wales or Northern Ireland ;

(*b*) a judgment given in proceedings other than civil proceedings ;

(*c*) a judgment given in proceedings relating to—

(i) bankruptcy ; or

(ii) the winding up of a corporation or association ; or

(iii) the obtaining of title to administer the estate of a deceased person.

(4) This section applies, whatever the nature of the proceedings in which it is made, to—

(*a*) a decree issued under section 13 of the Court of Exchequer (Scotland) Act 1856 (recovery of certain rentcharges and penalties by process of the Court of Session) ; 1856 c. 56.

(*b*) an order which is enforceable in the same manner as a judgment of the High Court in England and Wales by virtue of section 16 of the Contempt of Court Act 1981 or section 140 of the Supreme Court Act 1981 (which relate to fines for contempt of court and forfeiture of recognisances). 1981 c. 49. 1981 c. 54.

(5) This section does not apply to so much of any judgment as—

(*a*) is an order to which section 16 of the Maintenance Orders Act 1950 applies (and is therefore an order for whose enforcement in another part of the United Kingdom provision is made by Part II of that Act) ; 1950 c. 37

PART II

(*b*) concerns the status or legal capacity of an individual;

(*c*) relates to the management of the affairs of a person not capable of managing his own affairs;

(*d*) is a provisional (including protective) measure other than an order for the making of an interim payment;

and except where otherwise stated references to a judgment to which this section applies are to such a judgment exclusive of any such provisions.

(6) The following are within subsection (5)(*b*), but without prejudice to the generality of that provision—

(*a*) a decree of judicial separation or of separation;

(*b*) any provision relating to guardianship or custody.

(7) This section does not apply to a judgment of a court outside the United Kingdom which falls to be treated for the purposes of its enforcement as a judgment of a court of law in the United Kingdom by virtue of registration under Part II of the Administration of Justice Act 1920, Part I of the Foreign Judgments (Reciprocal Enforcement) Act 1933, Part I of the Maintenance Orders (Reciprocal Enforcement) Act 1972 or section 4 or 5 of this Act.

1920 c. 81.
1933 c. 13.
1972 c. 18.

(8) A judgment to which this section applies, other than a judgment within paragraph (*e*) of subsection (2), shall not be enforced in another part of the United Kingdom except by way of registration under Schedule 6 or 7.

Recognition of U.K. judgments in other parts of U.K.

19.—(1) A judgment to which this section applies given in one part of the United Kingdom shall not be refused recognition in another part of the United Kingdom solely on the ground that, in relation to that judgment, the court which gave it was not a court of competent jurisdiction according to the rules of private international law in force in that other part.

(2) Subject to subsection (3), this section applies to any judgment to which section 18 applies.

(3) This section does not apply to—

(*a*) the documents mentioned in paragraph (*c*) of the definition of " judgment " in section 18(2);

(*b*) the awards and orders mentioned in paragraphs (*d*) and (*e*) of that definition;

(*c*) the decrees and orders referred to in section 18(4);

PART III

JURISDICTION IN SCOTLAND

Rules as to jurisdiction in Scotland.

20.—(1) Subject to Parts I and II and to the following provisions of this Part, Schedule 8 has effect to determine in what circumstances a person may be sued in civil proceedings in the Court of Session or in a sheriff court.

(2) Nothing in Schedule 8 affects the competence as respects subject-matter or value of the Court of Session or of the sheriff court.

(3) Section 6 of the Sheriff Courts (Scotland) Act 1907 shall cease to have effect to the extent that it determines jurisdiction in relation to any matter to which Schedule 8 applies. 1907 c. 51.

(4) In Schedule 8—

(*a*) words resulting from modifications of Title II of the 1968 Convention, by way of addition or substitution, and provisions not derived from that Title are printed in heavy type; and

(*b*) the marginal notes show, where appropriate, of which provision of Title II a provision of Schedule 8 is a modified version.

(5) In determining any question as to the meaning or effect of any provision contained in Schedule 8 and derived to any extent from Title II of the 1968 Convention—

(*a*) regard shall be had to any relevant principles laid down by the European Court in connection with Title II of the 1968 Convention and to any relevant decision of that court as to the meaning or effect of any provision of that Title; and

(*b*) without prejudice to the generality of paragraph (*a*), the reports mentioned in section 3(3) may be considered and shall, so far as relevant, be given such weight as is appropriate in the circumstances.

Continuance of certain existing jurisdictions.

21.—(1) Schedule 8 does not affect—

(*a*) the operation of any enactment which confers jurisdiction on a Scottish court in respect of a specific subject-matter on specific grounds;

(*b*) without prejudice to the foregoing generality, the jurisdiction of any court in respect of any matter mentioned in Schedule 9.

(2) Her Majesty may by Order in Council—

(*a*) add to the list in Schedule 9 any description of proceedings; and

(*b*) remove from that list any description of proceedings (whether included in the list as originally enacted or added by virtue of this subsection).

PART III

(3) An Order in Council under subsection (2) may—

(*a*) make different provision for different descriptions of proceedings or for the same description of proceedings in different courts; and

(*b*) contain such transitional and other incidental provisions as appear to Her Majesty to be appropriate.

(4) An Order in Council under subsection (2) shall not be made unless a draft of the Order has been laid before Parliament and approved by a resolution of each House of Parliament.

Supplementary provisions.

22.—(1) Nothing in Schedule 8 shall prevent a court from declining jurisdiction on the ground of *forum non conveniens.*

(2) Nothing in Schedule 8 affects the operation of any enactment or rule of law under which a court may decline to exercise jurisdiction because of the prorogation by parties of the jurisdiction of another court.

(3) For the avoidance of doubt, it is declared that nothing in Schedule 8 affects the *nobile officium* of the Court of Session.

(4) Where a court has jurisdiction in any proceedings by virtue of Schedule 8, that court shall also have jurisdiction to determine any matter which—

(*a*) is ancilliary or incidental to the proceedings; or

(*b*) requires to be determined for the purposes of a decision in the proceedings.

Savings and consequential amendments.

23.—(1) Nothing in Schedule 8 shall affect—

(*a*) the power of any court to vary or recall a maintenance order granted by that court;

(*b*) the power of a sheriff court under section 22 of the
1950 c. 37 Maintenance Orders Act 1950 (discharge and variation of maintenance orders registered in sheriff courts) to vary or discharge a maintenance order registered in that court under Part II of that Act; or

(*c*) the power of a sheriff court under section 9 of the
1972 c. 18. Maintenance Orders (Reciprocal Enforcement) Act 1972 (variation and revocation of maintenance orders registered in United Kingdom courts) to vary or revoke a registered order within the meaning of Part I of that Act.

(2) The enactments specified in Part II of Schedule 12 shall have effect with the amendments specified there, being amendments consequential on Schedule 8.

PART IV

MISCELLANEOUS PROVISIONS

Provisions relating to jurisdiction

Interim relief and protective measures in cases of doubtful jurisdiction.

24.—(1) Any power of a court in England and Wales or Northern Ireland to grant interim relief pending trial or pending the determination of an appeal shall extend to a case where—

(*a*) the issue to be tried, or which is the subject of the appeal, relates to the jurisdiction of the court to entertain the proceedings; or

(*b*) the proceedings involve the reference of any matter to the European Court under the 1971 Protocol.

(2) Any power of a court in Scotland to grant protective measures pending the decision of any hearing shall apply to a case where—

(*a*) the subject of the proceedings includes a question as to the jurisdiction of the court to entertain them; or

(*b*) the proceedings involve the reference of a matter to the European Court under the 1971 Protocol.

(3) Subsections (1) and (2) shall not be construed as restricting any power to grant interim relief or protective measures which a court may have apart from this section.

Interim relief in England and Wales and Northern Ireland in the absence of substantive proceedings.

25.—(1) The High Court in England and Wales or Northern Ireland shall have power to grant interim relief where—

(*a*) proceedings have been or are to be commenced in a Contracting State other than the United Kingdom or in a part of the United Kingdom other than that in which the High Court in question exercises jurisdiction; and

(*b*) they are or will be proceedings whose subject-matter is within the scope of the 1968 Convention as determined by Article 1 (whether or not the Convention has effect in relation to the proceedings).

(2) On an application for any interim relief under subsection (1) the court may refuse to grant that relief if, in the opinion of the court, the fact that the court has no jurisdiction apart from this section in relation to the subject-matter of the proceedings in question makes it inexpedient for the court to grant it.

(3) Her Majesty may by Order in Council extend the power to grant interim relief conferred by subsection (1) so as to make it exercisable in relation to proceedings of any of the following descriptions, namely—

(*a*) proceedings commenced or to be commenced otherwise than in a Contracting State;

PART IV

(*b*) proceedings whose subject-matter is not within the scope of the 1968 Convention as determined by Article 1;

(*c*) arbitration proceedings.

(4) An Order in Council under subsection (3)—

(*a*) may confer power to grant only specified descriptions of interim relief;

(*b*) may make different provision for different classes of proceedings, for proceedings pending in different countries or courts outside the United Kingdom or in different parts of the United Kingdom, and for other different circumstances; and

(*c*) may impose conditions or restrictions on the exercise of any power conferred by the Order.

(5) An Order in Council under subsection (3) which confers power to grant interim relief in relation to arbitration proceedings may provide for the repeal of any provision of section 12(6) of the Arbitration Act 1950 or section 21(1) of the Arbitration Act (Northern Ireland) 1937 to the extent that it is superseded by the provisions of the Order.

1950 c. 27. 1937 c. 8. (N.I.).

(6) Any Order in Council under subsection (3) shall be subject to annulment in pursuance of a resolution of either House of Parliament.

(7) In this section " interim relief ", in relation to the High Court in England and Wales or Northern Ireland, means interim relief of any kind which that court has power to grant in proceedings relating to matters within its jurisdiction, other than—

(*a*) a warrant for the arrest of property; or

(*b*) provision for obtaining evidence.

Security in Admiralty proceedings in England and Wales or Northern Ireland in case of stay, etc.

26.—(1) Where in England and Wales or Northern Ireland a court stays or dismisses Admiralty proceedings on the ground that the dispute in question should be submitted to arbitration or to the determination of the courts of another part of the United Kingdom or of an overseas country, the court may, if in those proceedings property has been arrested or bail or other security has been given to prevent or obtain release from arrest—

(*a*) order that the property arrested be retained as security for the satisfaction of any award or judgment which—

(i) is given in respect of the dispute in the arbitration or legal proceedings in favour of which those proceedings are stayed or dismissed; and

(ii) is enforceable in England and Wales or, as the case may be, in Northern Ireland; or (*b*) order that the stay or dismissal of those proceedings be conditional on the provision of equivalent security for the satisfaction of any such award or judgment.

(2) Where a court makes an order under subsection (1), it may attach such conditions to the order as it thinks fit, in particular conditions with respect to the institution or prosecution of the relevant arbitration or legal proceedings.

(3) Subject to any provision made by rules of court and to any necessary modifications, the same law and practice shall apply in relation to property retained in pursuance of an order made by a court under subsection (1) as would apply if it were held for the purposes of proceedings in that court.

Provisional and protective measures in Scotland in the absence of substantive proceedings.

27.—(1) The Court of Session may, in any case to which this subsection applies—

(*a*) subject to subsection (2)(*c*), grant a warrant for the arrestment of any assets situated in Scotland ;

(*b*) subject to subsection (2)(*c*), grant a warrant of inhibition over any property situated in Scotland ; and

(*c*) grant interim interdict.

(2) Subsection (1) applies to any case in which—

(*a*) proceedings have been commenced but not concluded, or, in relation to paragraph (*c*) of that subsection, are to be commenced, in another Contracting State or in England and Wales or Northern Ireland ;

(*b*) the subject-matter of the proceedings is within the scope of the 1968 Convention as determined by Article 1 ; and

(*c*) in relation to paragraphs (*a*) and (*b*) of subsection (1), such a warrant could competently have been granted in equivalent proceedings before a Scottish court ;

but it shall not be necessary, in determining whether proceedings have been commenced for the purpose of paragraph (*a*) of this subsection, to show that any document has been served on or notice given to the defender.

(3) Her Majesty may by Order in Council confer on the Court of Session power to do anything mentioned in subsection (1) or in section 28 in relation to proceedings of any of the following descriptions, namely—

(*a*) proceedings commenced otherwise than in a Contracting State ;

(*b*) proceedings whose subject-matter is not within the scope of the 1968 Convention as determined by Article 1 ;

(*c*) arbitration proceedings ;

PART IV

(*d*) in relation to subsection (1)(*c*) or section 28, proceedings which are to be commenced otherwise than in a Contracting State.

(4) An Order in Council under subsection (3)—

(*a*) may confer power to do only certain of the things mentioned in subsection (1) or in section 28 ;

(*b*) may make different provision for different classes of proceedings, for proceedings pending in different countries or courts outside the United Kingdom or in different parts of the United Kingdom, and for other different circumstances ; and

(*c*) may impose conditions or restrictions on the exercise of any power conferred by the Order.

(5) Any Order in Council under subsection (3) shall be subject to annulment in pursuance of a resolution of either House of Parliament.

Application of s. 1 of Administration of Justice (Scotland) Act 1972.
1972 c. 59.

28. When any proceedings have been brought, or are likely to be brought, in another Contracting State or in England and Wales or Northern Ireland in respect of any matter which is within the scope of the 1968 Convention as determined in Article 1, the Court of Session shall have the like power to make an order under section 1 of the Administration of Justice (Scotland) Act 1972 as if the proceedings in question had been brought, or were likely to be brought, in that court.

Service of county court process outside Northern Ireland.
S.I. 1980/397 (N.I. 3).

29. The County Court Rules Committee established by Article 46 of the County Courts (Northern Ireland) Order 1980 may make county court rules with respect to the service of process outside Northern Ireland and the conditions subject to which process may be so served ; and accordingly in Article 48 of that Order (powers of Rules Committee), after paragraph (*e*) there shall be added—

" (*f*) the service of process outside Northern Ireland, and the conditions subject to which process may be so served.".

Proceedings in England and Wales or Northern Ireland for torts to immovable property.

30.—(1) The jurisdiction of any court in England and Wales or Northern Ireland to entertain proceedings for trespass to, or any other tort affecting, immovable property shall extend to cases in which the property in question is situated outside that part of the United Kingdom unless the proceedings are principally concerned with a question of the title to, or the right to possession of, that property.

(2) Subsection (1) has effect subject to the 1968 Convention and to the provisions set out in Schedule 4.

PART IV

Provisions relating to recognition and enforcement of judgments

31.—(1) A judgment given by a court of an overseas country against a state other than the United Kingdom or the state to which that court belongs shall be recognised and enforced in the United Kingdom if, and only if— Overseas judgments given against states, etc.

(*a*) it would be so recognised and enforced if it had not been given against a state ; and

(*b*) that court would have had jurisdiction in the matter if it had applied rules corresponding to those applicable to such matters in the United Kingdom in accordance with sections 2 to 11 of the State Immunity Act 1978. 1978 c. 33.

(2) References in subsection (1) to a judgment given against a state include references to judgments of any of the following descriptions given in relation to a state—

(*a*) judgments against the government, or a department of the government, of the state but not (except as mentioned in paragraph (*c*)) judgments against an entity which is distinct from the executive organs of government ;

(*b*) judgments against the sovereign or head of state in his public capacity ;

(*c*) judgments against any such separate entity as is mentioned in paragraph (*a*) given in proceedings relating to anything done by it in the exercise of the sovereign authority of the state.

(3) Nothing in subsection (1) shall affect the recognition or enforcement in the United Kingdom of a judgment to which Part I of the Foreign Judgments (Reciprocal Enforcement) Act 1933 applies by virtue of section 4 of the Carriage of Goods by Road Act 1965, section 17(4) of the Nuclear Installations Act 1965, section 13(3) of the Merchant Shipping (Oil Pollution) Act 1971, section 5 of the Carriage by Railway Act 1972 or section 5 of the Carriage of Passengers by Road Act 1974. 1933 c. 13. 1965 c. 37. 1965 c. 57. 1971 c. 59. 1972 c. 33. 1974 c. 35.

(4) Sections 12, 13 and 14(3) and (4) of the State Immunity Act 1978 (service of process and procedural privileges) shall apply to proceedings for the recognition or enforcement in the United Kingdom of a judgment given by a court of an overseas country (whether or not that judgment is within subsection (1) of this section) as they apply to other proceedings.

(5) In this section " state ", in the case of a federal state, includes any of its constituent territories.

PART IV

Overseas judgments given in proceedings brought in breach of agreement for settlement of disputes.

32.—(1) Subject to the following provisions of this section, a judgment given by a court of an overseas country in any proceedings shall not be recognised or enforced in the United Kingdom if—

(*a*) the bringing of those proceedings in that court was contrary to an agreement under which the dispute in question was to be settled otherwise than by proceedings in the courts of that country; and

(*b*) those proceedings were not brought in that court by, or with the agreement of, the person against whom the judgment was given; and

(*c*) that person did not counterclaim in the proceedings or otherwise submit to the jurisdiction of that court.

(2) Subsection (1) does not apply where the agreement referred to in paragraph (*a*) of that subsection was illegal, void or unenforceable or was incapable of being performed for reasons not attributable to the fault of the party bringing the proceedings in which the judgment was given.

(3) In determining whether a judgment given by a court of an overseas country should be recognised or enforced in the United Kingdom, a court in the United Kingdom shall not be bound by any decision of the overseas court relating to any of the matters mentioned in subsection (1) or (2).

(4) Nothing in subsection (1) shall affect the recognition or enforcement in the United Kingdom of—

(*a*) a judgment which is required to be recognised or enforced there under the 1968 Convention;

1933 c. 13. 1965 c. 37. 1965 c. 57. 1971 c. 59. 1972 c. 33. 1974 c. 35. 1974 c. 43.

(*b*) a judgment to which Part I of the Foreign Judgments (Reciprocal Enforcement) Act 1933 applies by virtue of section 4 of the Carriage of Goods by Road Act 1965, section 17(4) of the Nuclear Installations Act 1965, section 13(3) of the Merchant Shipping (Oil Pollution) Act 1971, section 5 of the Carriage by Railway Act 1972, section 5 of the Carriage of Passengers by Road Act 1974 or section 6(4) of the Merchant Shipping Act 1974.

Certain steps not to amount to submission to jurisdiction of overseas court.

33.—(1) For the purposes of determining whether a judgment given by a court of an overseas country should be recognised or enforced in England and Wales or Northern Ireland, the person against whom the judgment was given shall not be regarded as having submitted to the jurisdiction of the court by reason only of the fact that he appeared (conditionally or otherwise) in the proceedings for all or any one or more of the following purposes, namely—

(*a*) to contest the jurisdiction of the court;

PART IV

(*b*) to ask the court to dismiss or stay the proceedings on the ground that the dispute in question should be submitted to arbitration or to the determination of the courts of another country ;

(*c*) to protect, or obtain the release of, property seized or threatened with seizure in the proceedings.

(2) Nothing in this section shall affect the recognition or enforcement in England and Wales or Northern Ireland of a judgment which is required to be recognised or enforced there under the 1968 Convention.

Certain judgments a bar to further proceedings on the same cause of action.

34. No proceedings may be brought by a person in England and Wales or Northern Ireland on a cause of action in respect of which a judgment has been given in his favour in proceedings between the same parties, or their privies, in a court in another part of the United Kingdom or in a court of an overseas country, unless that judgment is not enforceable or entitled to recognition in England and Wales or, as the case may be, in Northern Ireland.

Minor amendments relating to overseas judgments. 1933 c. 13.

35.—(1) The Foreign Judgments (Reciprocal Enforcement) Act 1933 shall have effect with the amendments specified in Schedule 10, being amendments whose main purpose is to enable Part I of that Act to be applied to judgments of courts other than superior courts, to judgments providing for interim payments and to certain arbitration awards.

1920 c. 81.

(2) For section 10 of the Administration of Justice Act 1920 (issue of certificates of judgments obtained in the United Kingdom) there shall be substituted—

" 10.—(1) Where—

(*a*) a judgment has been obtained in the High Court in England or Northern Ireland, or in the Court of Session in Scotland, against any person ; and

(*b*) the judgment creditor wishes to secure the enforcement of the judgment in a part of Her Majesty's dominions outside the United Kingdom to which this Part of this Act extends,

the court shall, on an application made by the judgment creditor, issue to him a certified copy of the judgment.

PART IV

(2) The reference in the preceding subsection to Her Majesty's dominions shall be construed as if that subsection had come into force in its present form at the commencement of this Act. ".

1920 c. 81.

(3) In section 14 of the Administration of Justice Act 1920 (extent of Part II of that Act), after subsection (2) there shall be inserted—

" (3) Her Majesty may by Order in Council under this section consolidate any Orders in Council under this section which are in force when the consolidating Order is made.".

Registration of maintenance orders in Northern Ireland.

1950 c. 37.

36.—(1) Where—

(*a*) a High Court order or a Court of Session order has been registered in the High Court of Justice in Northern Ireland (" the Northern Ireland High Court ") under Part II of the Maintenance Orders Act 1950 ; or

(*b*) a county court order, a magistrates' court order or a sheriff court order has been registered in a court of summary jurisdiction in Northern Ireland under that Part,

an application may be made to the original court for the registration of the order in, respectively, a court of summary jurisdiction in Northern Ireland or the Northern Ireland High Court.

(2) In subsection (1) " the original court ", in relation to an order, means the court by which the order was made.

1958 c. 39.

(3) Section 2 (except subsection (6A)) and section 2A of the Maintenance Orders Act 1958 shall have effect for the purposes of an application under subsection (1), and subsections (2), (3), (4) and (4A) of section 5 of that Act shall have effect for the purposes of the cancellation of a registration made on such an application, as if—

(*a*) " registration " in those provisions included registration in the appropriate Northern Ireland court (" registered " being construed accordingly) ;

(*b*) any reference in those provisions to a High Court order or a magistrates' court order included, respectively, a Court of Session order or a sheriff court order ; and

(*c*) any other reference in those provisions to the High Court or a magistrates' court included the Northern Ireland High Court or a court of summary jurisdiction in Northern Ireland.

1966 c. 35. (N.I.)

(4) Where an order is registered in Northern Ireland under this section, Part II of the Maintenance and Affiliation Orders Act (Northern Ireland) 1966, except sections 11, 11A and 14(2) and (3), shall apply as if the order had been registered in accordance with the provisions of that Part.

Part IV

(5) A court of summary jurisdiction in Northern Ireland shall have jurisdiction to hear a complaint by or against a person residing outside Northern Ireland for the discharge or variation of an order registered in Northern Ireland under this section; and where such a complaint is made against a person residing outside Northern Ireland, then, if he resides in England and Wales or Scotland, section 15 of the Maintenance Orders Act 1950 (which relates to the service of process on persons residing in those countries) shall have effect in relation to the complaint as it has effect in relation to the proceedings therein mentioned. **1950 c. 37.**

(6) The enactments specified in Part III of Schedule 12 shall have effect with the amendments specified there, being amendments consequential on this section.

Minor amendments relating to maintenance orders.

37.—(1) The enactments specified in Schedule 11 shall have effect with the amendments specified there, being amendments whose main purpose is as follows—

Part I—to extend certain enforcement provisions to lump sum maintenance orders;

Part II—to provide for the recovery of interest according to the law of the country of origin in the case of maintenance orders made in other jurisdictions and registered in the High Court;

Part III—to extend the Maintenance Orders (Reciprocal Enforcement) Act 1972 to cases where the payer under a maintenance order is not resident within the jurisdiction but has assets there. 1972 c. 18.

(2) In section 27(1) of the Maintenance Orders (Reciprocal Enforcement) Act 1972 (application by person in convention country for recovery of maintenance in England and Wales or Northern Ireland to be treated as a complaint), after " as if it were a complaint " there shall be inserted " made at the time when the application was received by the Secretary of State or the Lord Chancellor ".

Overseas judgments counteracting an award of multiple damages.

38.—(1) Section 7 of the Protection of Trading Interests Act 1980 (which enables provision to be made by Order in Council for the enforcement in the United Kingdom on a reciprocal basis of overseas judgments directed to counteracting a judgment for multiple damages given in a third country) shall be amended as follows. **1980 c. 11.**

(2) In subsection (1) for " judgments given under any provision of the law of that country corresponding to that section " there shall be substituted " judgments of any description specified in the Order which are given under any provision of the law of that

PART IV

country relating to the recovery of sums paid or obtained pursuant to a judgment for multiple damages within the meaning of section 5(3) above, whether or not that provision corresponds to section 6 above ".

(3) After subsection (1) there shall be inserted—

" (1A) Such an Order in Council may, as respects judgments to which it relates—

(*a*) make different provisions for different descriptions of judgment; and

(*b*) impose conditions or restrictions on the enforcement of judgments of any description.".

Jurisdiction, and recognition and enforcement of judgments, as between United Kingdom and certain territories

Application of provisions corresponding to 1968 Convention in relation to certain territories.

39.—(1) Her Majesty may by Order in Council make provision corresponding to the provision made by the 1968 Convention as between the Contracting States to that Convention, with such modifications as appear to Her Majesty to be appropriate, for regulating, as between the United Kingdom and any of the territories mentioned in subsection (2), the jurisdiction of courts and the recognition and enforcement of judgments.

(2) The territories referred to in subsection (1) are—

(*a*) the Isle of Man;

(*b*) any of the Channel Islands;

(*c*) Gibraltar;

(*d*) the Sovereign Base Areas of Akrotiri and Dhekelia (that is to say the areas mentioned in section 2(1) of the Cyprus Act 1960).

1960 c. 52.

(3) An Order in Council under this section may contain such supplementary and incidental provisions as appear to Her Majesty to be necessary or expedient, including in particular provisions corresponding to or applying any of the provisions of Part I with such modifications as may be specified in the Order.

(4) Any Order in Council under this section shall be subject to annulment in pursuance of a resolution of either House of Parliament.

Legal aid

Power to modify enactments relating to legal aid etc.

1974 c. 4.

40.—(1) In section 20 of the Legal Aid Act 1974 (power of Lord Chancellor to make regulations), after subsection (4) there shall be inserted as subsection (4A)—

" (4A) Without prejudice to the preceding provisions of this section or any other provision of this Part of this Act authorising the making of regulations, regulations may also modify the provisions of, or of any instrument having effect under, this Part of this Act (including so much of any of those provisions as specifies a sum of money) for the purposes of the application of those provisions— PART IV

(*a*) in cases where their modification appears to the Lord Chancellor necessary for the purpose of fulfilling any obligation imposed on the United Kingdom or Her Majesty's government therein by any international agreement ; or

(*b*) in relation to proceedings for securing the recognition or enforcement in England and Wales of judgments given outside the United Kingdom for whose recognition or enforcement in the United Kingdom provision is made by any international agreement.".

(2) In section 15 of the Legal Aid (Scotland) Act 1967 (power of Secretary of State to make regulations), after subsection (4) there shall be inserted as subsection (4A)— 1967 c. 43.

" (4A) Without prejudice to the preceding provisions of this section or any other provision of this Act authorising the making of regulations, regulations may also modify the provisions of, or of any instrument having effect under, this Act (including so much of any of those provisions as specifies a sum of money) for the purposes of the application of those provisions—

(*a*) in cases where their modification appears to the Secretary of State necessary for the purpose of fulfilling any obligation imposed on the United Kingdom or Her Majesty's government therein by any international agreement ; or

(*b*) in relation to proceedings for securing the recognition or enforcement in Scotland of judgments given outside the United Kingdom for whose recognition or enforcement in the United Kingdom provision is made by any international agreement.".

(3) In Article 22 of the Legal Aid, Advice and Assistance (Northern Ireland) Order 1981 (power of Lord Chancellor to make regulations), after paragraph (4) there shall be inserted as paragraph (4A)— S.I. 1981/228 (N.I. 8).

" (4A) Without prejudice to the preceding provisions of this Article or any other provision of this Part authorising the making of regulations, regulations may also modify the provisions of, or of any instrument having effect under, this Part (including so much of any of those provisions as specifies a sum of money) for the purposes of the application of those provisions—

(*a*) in cases where their modification appears to the Lord Chancellor necessary for the purpose of

PART IV

fulfilling any obligation imposed on the United Kingdom or Her Majesty's government therein by any international agreement ; or

(*b*) in relation to proceedings for securing the recognition or enforcement in Northern Ireland of judgments given outside the United Kingdom for whose recognition or enforcement in the United Kingdom provision is made by any international agreement.".

PART V

SUPPLEMENTARY AND GENERAL PROVISIONS

Domicile

Domicile of individuals.

41.—(1) Subject to Article 52 (which contains provisions for determining whether a party is domiciled in a Contracting State), the following provisions of this section determine, for the purposes of the 1968 Convention and this Act, whether an individual is domiciled in the United Kingdom or in a particular part of, or place in, the United Kingdom or in a state other than a Contracting State.

(2) An individual is domiciled in the United Kingdom if and only if—

(*a*) he is resident in the United Kingdom ; and

(*b*) the nature and circumstances of his residence indicate that he has a substantial connection with the United Kingdom.

(3) Subject to subsection (5), an individual is domiciled in a particular part of the United Kingdom if and only if—

(*a*) he is resident in that part ; and

(*b*) the nature and circumstances of his residence indicate that he has a substantial connection with that part.

(4) An individual is domiciled in a particular place in the United Kingdom if and only if he—

(*a*) is domiciled in the part of the United Kingdom in which that place is situated ; and

(*b*) is resident in that place.

(5) An individual who is domiciled in the United Kingdom but in whose case the requirements of subsection (3)(*b*) are not satisfied in relation to any particular part of the United Kingdom shall be treated as domiciled in the part of the United Kingdom in which he is resident.

(6) In the case of an individual who—

(*a*) is resident in the United Kingdom, or in a particular part of the United Kingdom ; and

(b) has been so resident for the last three months or more,

the requirements of subsection (2)(b) or, as the case may be, subsection (3)(b) shall be presumed to be fulfilled unless the contrary is proved.

(7) An individual is domiciled in a state other than a Contracting State if and only if—

(a) he is resident in that state; and

(b) the nature and circumstances of his residence indicate that he has a substantial connection with that state.

Domicile and seat of corporation or association.

42.—(1) For the purposes of this Act the seat of a corporation or association (as determined by this section) shall be treated as its domicile.

(2) The following provisions of this section determine where a corporation or association has its seat—

(a) for the purpose of Article 53 (which for the purposes of the 1968 Convention equates the domicile of such a body with its seat); and

(b) for the purposes of this Act other than the provisions mentioned in section 43(1)(b) and (c).

(3) A corporation or association has its seat in the United Kingdom if and only if—

(a) it was incorporated or formed under the law of a part of the United Kingdom and has its registered office or some other official address in the United Kingdom; or

(b) its central management and control is exercised in the United Kingdom.

(4) A corporation or association has its seat in a particular part of the United Kingdom if and only if it has its seat in the United Kingdom and—

(a) it has its registered office or some other official address in that part; or

(b) its central management and control is exercised in that part; or

(c) it has a place of business in that part.

(5) A corporation or association has its seat in a particular place in the United Kingdom if and only if it has its seat in the part of the United Kingdom in which that place is situated and—

(a) it has its registered office or some other official address in that place; or

(b) its central management and control is exercised in that place; or

PART V

(*c*) it has a place of business in that place.

(6) Subject to subsection (7), a corporation or association has its seat in a state other than the United Kingdom if and only if—

(*a*) it was incorporated or formed under the law of that state and has its registered office or some other official address there ; or

(*b*) its central management and control is exercised in that state.

(7) A corporation or association shall not be regarded as having its seat in a Contracting State other than the United Kingdom if it is shown that the courts of that state would not regard it as having its seat there.

(8) In this section—

" business " includes any activity carried on by a corporation or association, and " place of business " shall be construed accordingly ;

" official address ", in relation to a corporation or association, means an address which it is required by law to register, notify or maintain for the purpose of receiving notices or other communications.

Seat of corporation or association for purposes of Article 16(2) and related provisions.

43.—(1) The following provisions of this section determine where a corporation or association has its seat for the purposes of—

(*a*) Article 16(2) (which confers exclusive jurisdiction over proceedings relating to the formation or dissolution of such bodies, or to the decisions of their organs) ;

(*b*) Articles 5A and 16(2) in Schedule 4 ; and

(*c*) Rules 2(12) and 4(1)(*b*) in Schedule 8.

(2) A corporation or association has its seat in the United Kingdom if and only if—

(*a*) it was incorporated or formed under the law of a part of the United Kingdom ; or

(*b*) its central management and control is exercised in the United Kingdom.

(3) A corporation or association has its seat in a particular part of the United Kingdom if and only if it has its seat in the United Kingdom and—

(*a*) subject to subsection (5), it was incorporated or formed under the law of that part ; or

(*b*) being incorporated or formed under the law of a state other than the United Kingdom, its central management and control is exercised in that part.

(4) A corporation or association has its seat in a particular place in Scotland if and only if it has its seat in Scotland and—

(a) it has its registered office or some other official address in that place ; or

(b) it has no registered office or other official address in Scotland, but its central management and control is exercised in that place.

(5) A corporation or association incorporated or formed under—

(a) an enactment forming part of the law of more than one part of the United Kingdom ; or

(b) an instrument having effect in the domestic law of more than one part of the United Kingdom,

shall, if it has a registered office, be taken to have its seat in the part of the United Kingdom in which that office is situated, and not in any other part of the United Kingdom.

(6) Subject to subsection (7), a corporation or association has its seat in a Contracting State other than the United Kingdom if and only if—

(a) it was incorporated or formed under the law of that state ; or

(b) its central management and control is exercised in that state.

(7) A corporation or association shall not be regarded as having its seat in a Contracting State other than the United Kingdom if—

(a) it has its seat in the United Kingdom by virtue of subsection (2)(a) ; or

(b) it is shown that the courts of that other state would not regard it for the purposes of Article 16(2) as having its seat there.

(8) In this section " official address " has the same meaning as in section 42.

Persons deemed to be domiciled in the United Kingdom for certain purposes.

44.—(1) This section applies to—

(a) proceedings within Section 3 of Title II of the 1968 Convention (insurance contracts), and

(b) proceedings within Section 4 of that Title (consumer contracts).

(2) A person who, for the purposes of proceedings to which this section applies arising out of the operations of a branch, agency or other establishment in the United Kingdom, is deemed for the purposes of the 1968 Convention to be domiciled in the United Kingdom by virtue of—

(a) Article 8, second paragraph (insurers) ; or

PART V

(*b*) Article 13, second paragraph (suppliers of goods, services or credit to consumers),

shall, for the purposes of those proceedings, be treated for the purposes of this Act as so domiciled and as domiciled in the part of the United Kingdom in which the branch, agency or establishment in question is situated.

Domicile of trusts.

45.—(1) The following provisions of this section determine, for the purposes of the 1968 Convention and this Act, where a trust is domiciled.

(2) A trust is domiciled in the United Kingdom if and only if it is by virtue of subsection (3) domiciled in a part of the United Kingdom.

(3) A trust is domiciled in a part of the United Kingdom if and only if the system of law of that part is the system of law with which the trust has its closest and most real connection.

Domicile and seat of the Crown.

46.—(1) For the purposes of this Act the seat of the Crown (as determined by this section) shall be treated as its domicile.

(2) The following provisions of this section determine where the Crown has its seat—

(*a*) for the purposes of the 1968 Convention (in which Article 53 equates the domicile of a legal person with its seat); and

(*b*) for the purposes of this Act.

(3) Subject to the provisions of any Order in Council for the time being in force under subsection (4)—

(*a*) the Crown in right of Her Majesty's government in the United Kingdom has its seat in every part of, and every place in, the United Kingdom; and

(*b*) the Crown in right of Her Majesty's government in Northern Ireland has its seat in, and in every place in, Northern Ireland.

(4) Her Majesty may by Order in Council provide that, in the case of proceedings of any specified description against the Crown in right of Her Majesty's government in the United Kingdom, the Crown shall be treated for the purposes of the 1968 Convention and this Act as having its seat in, and in every place in, a specified part of the United Kingdom and not in any other part of the United Kingdom.

(5) An Order in Council under subsection (4) may frame a description of proceedings in any way, and in particular may do so by reference to the government department or officer of the Crown against which or against whom they fall to be instituted.

(6) Any Order in Council made under this section shall be subject to annulment in pursuance of a resolution of either House of Parliament.

(7) Nothing in this section applies to the Crown otherwise than in right of Her Majesty's government in the United Kingdom or Her Majesty's government in Northern Ireland.

Other supplementary provisions

Modifications occasioned by decisions of European Court as to meaning or effect of Conventions.

47.—(1) Her Majesty may by Order in Council—

(*a*) make such provision as Her Majesty considers appropriate for the purpose of bringing the law of any part of the United Kingdom into accord with the Conventions as affected by any principle laid down by the European Court in connection with the Conventions or by any decision of that court as to the meaning or effect of any provision of the Conventions ; or

(*b*) make such modifications of Schedule 4 or Schedule 8, or of any other statutory provision affected by any provision of either of those Schedules, as Her Majesty considers appropriate in view of any principle laid down by the European Court in connection with Title II of the 1968 Convention or of any decision of that court as to the meaning or effect of any provision of that Title.

(2) The provision which may be made by virtue of paragraph (*a*) of subsection (1) includes such modifications of this Act or any other statutory provision, whenever passed or made, as Her Majesty considers appropriate for the purpose mentioned in that paragraph.

(3) The modifications which may be made by virtue of paragraph (*b*) of subsection (1) include modifications designed to produce divergence between any provision of Schedule 4 or Schedule 8 and a corresponding provision of Title II of the 1968 Convention as affected by any such principle or decision as is mentioned in that paragraph.

(4) An Order in Council under this section shall not be made unless a draft of the Order has been laid before Parliament and approved by a resolution of each House of Parliament.

Matters for which rules of court may provide.

48.—(1) Rules of court may make provision for regulating the procedure to be followed in any court in connection with any provision of this Act or the Conventions.

(2) Rules of court may make provision as to the manner in which and the conditions subject to which a certificate or judgment registered in any court under any provision of this Act

PART V

may be enforced, including provision for enabling the court or, in Northern Ireland the Enforcement of Judgments Office, subject to any conditions specified in the rules, to give directions about such matters.

(3) Without prejudice to the generality of subsections (1) and (2), the power to make rules of court for magistrates' courts, and in Northern Ireland the power to make Judgment Enforcement Rules, shall include power to make such provision as the rule-making authority considers necessary or expedient for the purposes of the provisions of the Conventions and this Act relating to maintenance proceedings and the recognition and enforcement of maintenance orders, and shall in particular include power to make provision as to any of the following matters—

(*a*) authorising the service in another Contracting State of process issued by or for the purposes of a magistrates' court and the service and execution in England and Wales or Northern Ireland of process issued in another Contracting State ;

(*b*) requesting courts in other parts of the United Kingdom or in other Contracting States to take evidence there for the purposes of proceedings in England and Wales or Northern Ireland ;

(*c*) the taking of evidence in England and Wales or Northern Ireland in response to similar requests received from such courts ;

(*d*) the circumstances in which and the conditions subject to which any powers conferred under paragraphs (*a*) to (*c*) are to be exercised ;

(*e*) the admission in evidence, subject to such conditions as may be prescribed in the rules, of statements contained in documents purporting to be made or authenticated by a court in another part of the United Kingdom or in another Contracting State, or by a judge or official of such a court, which purport—

(i) to set out or summarise evidence given in proceedings in that court or to be documents received in evidence in such proceedings or copies of such documents ; or

(ii) to set out or summarise evidence taken for the purposes of proceedings in England and Wales or Northern Ireland, whether or not in response to any such request as is mentioned in paragraph (*b*) ; or

(iii) to record information relating to the payments made under an order of that court ;

(*f*) the circumstances and manner in which a magistrates' court may or must vary or revoke a maintenance order registered in that court, cancel the registration of, or refrain from enforcing, such an order or transmit such an order for enforcement in another part of the United Kingdom ; PART V

(*g*) the cases and manner in which courts in other parts of the United Kingdom or in other Contracting States are to be informed of orders made, or other things done, by or for the purposes of a magistrates' court ;

(*h*) the circumstances and manner in which a magistrates' court may communicate for other purposes with such courts ;

(*i*) the giving of notice of such matters as may be prescribed in the rules to such persons as may be so prescribed and the manner in which such notice is to be given.

(4) Nothing in this section shall be taken as derogating from the generality of any power to make rules of court conferred by any other enactment.

Saving for powers to stay, sist, strike out or dismiss proceedings.

49. Nothing in this Act shall prevent any court in the United Kingdom from staying, sisting, striking out or dismissing any proceedings before it, on the ground of *forum non conveniens* or otherwise, where to do so is not inconsistent with the 1968 Convention. Re Harrods (Buenos Aires)

General

Interpretation: general.

50. In this Act, unless the context otherwise requires—

" the Accession Convention " has the meaning given by section 1(1) ;

" Article " and references to sub-divisions of numbered Articles are to be construed in accordance with section 1(2)(*b*) ;

" association " means an unincorporated body of persons ;

" Contracting State " has the meaning given by section 1(3) ;

" the 1968 Convention " has the meaning given by section 1(1), and references to that Convention and to provisions of it are to be construed in accordance with section 1(2)(*a*) ;

" the Conventions " has the meaning given by section 1(1) ;

" corporation " means a body corporate, and includes a partnership subsisting under the law of Scotland ;

" court ", without more, includes a tribunal ;

PART V

" court of law ", in relation to the United Kingdom, means any of the following courts, namely—

(*a*) the House of Lords,

(*b*) in England and Wales or Northern Ireland, the Court of Appeal, the High Court, the Crown Court, a county court and a magistrates' court,

(*c*) in Scotland, the Court of Session and a sheriff court ;

" the Crown " is to be construed in accordance with section 51(2) ;

" enactment " includes an enactment comprised in Northern Ireland legislation ;

" judgment ", subject to sections 15(1) and 18(2) and to paragraph 1 of Schedules 6 and 7, means any judgment or order (by whatever name called) given or made by a court in any civil proceedings ;

" magistrates' court ", in relation to Northern Ireland, means a court of summary jurisdiction ;

" modifications " includes additions, omissions and alterations ;

" overseas country " means any country or territory outside the United Kingdom ;

" part of the United Kingdom " means England and Wales, Scotland or Northern Ireland ;

" the 1971 Protocol " has the meaning given by section 1(1), and references to that Protocol and to provisions of it are to be construed in accordance with section 1(2)(*a*) ;

" rules of court ", in relation to any court, means rules, orders or regulations made by the authority having power to make rules, orders or regulations regulating the procedure of that court, and includes—

(*a*) in Scotland, Acts of Sederunt ;

(*b*) in Northern Ireland, Judgment Enforcement Rules ;

" statutory provision " means any provision contained in an Act, or in any Northern Ireland legislation, or in—

(*a*) subordinate legislation (as defined in section 21(1) of the Interpretation Act 1978) ; or

1978 c. 30.

(*b*) any instrument of a legislative character made under any Northern Ireland legislation ;

" tribunal "—

(*a*) means a tribunal of any description other than a court of law ;

PART V

(*b*) in relation to an overseas country, includes, as regards matters relating to maintenance within the meaning of the 1968 Convention, any authority having power to give, enforce, vary or revoke a maintenance order.

Application to Crown.

51.—(1) This Act binds the Crown.

(2) In this section and elsewhere in this Act references to the Crown do not include references to Her Majesty in Her private capacity or to Her Majesty in right of Her Duchy of Lancaster or to the Duke of Cornwall.

Extent.

52.—(1) This Act extends to Northern Ireland.

(2) Without prejudice to the power conferred by section 39, Her Majesty may by Order in Council direct that all or any of the provisions of this Act apart from that section shall extend, subject to such modifications as may be specified in the Order, to any of the following territories, that is to say—

(*a*) the Isle of Man;

(*b*) any of the Channel Islands;

(*c*) Gibraltar;

(*d*) the Sovereign Base Areas of Akrotiri and Dhekelia (that is to say the areas mentioned in section 2(1) of the Cyprus Act 1960). 1960 c. 52.

Commencement, transitional provisions and savings.

53.—(1) This Act shall come into force in accordance with the provisions of Part I of Schedule 13.

(2) The transitional provisions and savings contained in Part II of that Schedule shall have effect in relation to the commencement of the provisions of this Act mentioned in that Part.

Repeals.

54. The enactments mentioned in Schedule 14 are hereby repealed to the extent specified in the third column of that Schedule.

Short title.

55. This Act may be cited as the Civil Jurisdiction and Judgments Act 1982.

SCHEDULES

Section 2(2).

SCHEDULE 1

Text of 1968 Convention, as Amended

ARRANGEMENT OF PROVISIONS

CONVENTION ON JURISDICTION AND THE ENFORCEMENT OF JUDGMENTS IN CIVIL AND COMMERCIAL MATTERS

Preamble

The High Contracting Parties to the Treaty establishing the European Economic Community,

Desiring to implement the provisions of Article 220 of that Treaty by virtue of which they undertook to secure the simplification of formalities governing the reciprocal recognition and enforcement of judgments of courts or tribunals;

Anxious to strengthen in the Community the legal protection of persons therein established;

Considering that it is necessary for this purpose to determine the international jurisdiction of their courts, to facilitate recognition and to introduce an expeditious procedure for securing the enforcement of judgments, authentic instruments and court settlements;

Have decided to conclude this Convention and to this end have designated as their Plenipotentiaries:

(Designations of Plenipotentiaries of the original six Contracting States)

Who, meeting within the Council, having exchanged their Full Powers, found in good and due form,

Have agreed as follows:

TITLE I

SCOPE

Article 1

This Convention shall apply in civil and commercial matters whatever the nature of the court or tribunal. It shall not extend, in particular, to revenue, customs or administrative matters.

The Convention shall not apply to:

(1) the status or legal capacity of natural persons, rights in property arising out of a matrimonial relationship, wills and succession;

(2) bankruptcy, proceedings relating to the winding-up of insolvent companies or other legal persons, judicial arrangements, compositions and analogous proceedings;

(3) social security;

(4) arbitration.

SCH. 1

TITLE II

JURISDICTION

Section 1

General provisions

ARTICLE 2

Subject to the provisions of this Convention, persons domiciled in a Contracting State shall, whatever their nationality, be sued in the courts of that State.

Persons who are not nationals of the State in which they are domiciled shall be governed by the rules of jurisdiction applicable to nationals of that State.

ARTICLE 3

Persons domiciled in a Contracting State may be sued in the courts of another Contracting State only by virtue of the rules set out in Sections 2 to 6 of this Title.

In particular the following provisions shall not be applicable as against them:

—in Belgium:	Article 15 of the civil code (*Code civil—Burgerlijk Wetboek)* and Article 638 of the Judicial code *(Code judiciaire—Gerechtelijk Wetboek)*;
—in Denmark:	Article 248(2) of the law on civil procedure *(Lov om rettens pleje)* and Chapter 3, Article 3 of the Greenland law on civil procedure (*Lov for Grønland om rettens pleje*);
—in the Federal Republic of Germany:	Article 23 of the code of civil procedure (*Zivilprozessordnung*);
—in France:	Articles 14 and 15 of the civil code *(Code civil)*;
—in Ireland:	the rules which enable jurisdiction to be founded on the document instituting the proceedings having been served on the defendant during his temporary presence in Ireland;
—in Italy:	Article 2 and Article 4, Nos 1 and 2 of the code of civil procedure (*Codice di procedura civile*);
—in Luxembourg:	Articles 14 and 15 of the civil code *(Code civil)*;

—in the Netherlands:	Article 126(3) and Article 127 of the code of civil procedure *(Wetboek van Burgerlijke Rechtsvordering)*;
—in the United Kingdom:	the rules which enable jurisdiction to be founded on: (*a*) the document instituting the proceedings having been served on the defendant during his temporary presence in the United Kingdom; or (*b*) the presence within the United Kingdom of property belonging to the defendant; or (*c*) the seizure by the plaintiff of property situated in the United Kingdom.

Article 4

If the defendant is not domiciled in a Contracting State, the jurisdiction of the courts of each Contracting State shall, subject to the provisions of Article 16, be determined by the law of that State.

As against such a defendant, any person domiciled in a Contracting State may, whatever his nationality, avail himself in that State of the rules of jurisdiction there in force, and in particular those specified in the second paragraph of Article 3, in the same way as the nationals of that State.

Section 2

Special jurisdiction

Article 5

A person domiciled in a Contracting State may, in another Contracting State, be sued:

(1) in matters relating to a contract, in the courts for the place of performance of the obligation in question;

(2) in matters relating to maintenance, in the courts for the place where the maintenance creditor is domiciled or habitually resident or, if the matter is ancillary to proceedings concerning the status of a person, in the court which, according to its own law, has jurisdiction to entertain those proceedings, unless that jurisdiction is based solely on the nationality of one of the parties;

(3) in matters relating to tort, delict or quasi-delict, in the courts for the place where the harmful event occurred;

SCH. 1

(4) as regards a civil claim for damages or restitution which is based on an act giving rise to criminal proceedings, in the court seised of those proceedings, to the extent that that court has jurisdiction under its own law to entertain civil proceedings;

(5) as regards a dispute arising out of the operations of a branch, agency or other establishment, in the courts for the place in which the branch, agency or other establishment is situated;

(6) in his capacity as settlor, trustee or beneficiary of a trust created by the operation of a statute, or by a written instrument, or created orally and evidenced in writing, in the courts of the Contracting State in which the trust is domiciled;

(7) as regards a dispute concerning the payment of remuneration claimed in respect of the salvage of a cargo or freight, in the court under the authority of which the cargo or freight in question:

(*a*) has been arrested to secure such payment, or

(*b*) could have been so arrested, but bail or other security has been given;

provided that this provision shall apply only if it is claimed that the defendant has an interest in the cargo or freight or had such an interest at the time of salvage.

ARTICLE 6

A person domiciled in a Contracting State may also be sued:

(1) where he is one of a number of defendants, in the courts for the place where any one of them is domiciled;

(2) as a third party in an action on a warranty or guarantee or in any other third party proceedings, in the court seised of the original proceedings, unless these were instituted solely with the object of removing him from the jurisdiction of the court which would be competent in his case;

(3) on a counterclaim arising from the same contract or facts on which the original claim was based, in the court in which the original claim is pending.

ARTICLE 6A

Where by virtue of this Convention a court of a Contracting State has jurisdiction in actions relating to liability arising from the use or operation of a ship, that court, or any other court substituted for this purpose by the internal law of that State, shall also have jurisdiction over claims for limitation of such liability.

Section 3

Jurisdiction in matters relating to insurance

Article 7

In matters relating to insurance, jurisdiction shall be determined by this Section, without prejudice to the provisions of Articles 4 and 5(5).

Article 8

An insurer domiciled in a Contracting State may be sued:

(1) in the courts of the State where he is domiciled, or

(2) in another Contracting State, in the courts for the place where the policy-holder is domiciled, or

(3) if he is a co-insurer, in the courts of a Contracting State in which proceedings are brought against the leading insurer.

An insurer who is not domiciled in a Contracting State but has a branch, agency or other establishment in one of the Contracting States shall, in disputes arising out of the operations of the branch, agency or establishment, be deemed to be domiciled in that State.

Article 9

In respect of liability insurance or insurance of immovable property, the insurer may in addition be sued in the courts for the place where the harmful event occurred. The same applies if movable and immovable property are covered by the same insurance policy and both are adversely affected by the same contingency.

Article 10

In respect of liability insurance, the insurer may also, if the law of the court permits it, be joined in proceedings which the injured party has brought against the insured.

The provisions of Articles 7, 8 and 9 shall apply to actions brought by the injured party directly against the insurer, where such direct actions are permitted.

If the law governing such direct actions provides that the policy-holder or the insured may be joined as a party to the action, the same court shall have jurisdiction over them.

Article 11

Without prejudice to the provisions of the third paragraph of Article 10, an insurer may bring proceedings only in the courts of the Contracting State in which the defendant is domiciled, irrespective of whether he is the policy-holder, the insured or a beneficiary.

SCH. 1

The provisions of this Section shall not affect the right to bring a counterclaim in the court in which, in accordance with this Section, the original claim is pending.

ARTICLE 12

The provisions of this Section may be departed from only by an agreement on jurisdiction:

(1) which is entered into after the dispute has arisen, or

(2) which allows the policy-holder, the insured or a beneficiary to bring proceedings in courts other than those indicated in this Section, or

(3) which is concluded between a policy-holder and an insurer, both of whom are at the time of conclusion of the contract domiciled or habitually resident in the same Contracting State, and which has the effect of conferring jurisdiction on the courts of that State even if the harmful event were to occur abroad, provided that such an agreement is not contrary to the law of that State, or

(4) which is concluded with a policy-holder who is not domiciled in a Contracting State, except in so far as the insurance is compulsory or relates to immovable property in a Contracting State, or

(5) which relates to a contract of insurance in so far as it covers one or more of the risks set out in Article 12A.

ARTICLE 12A

The following are the risks referred to in Article 12(5):

(1) Any loss of or damage to

(*a*) sea-going ships, installations situated offshore or on the high seas, or aircraft, arising from perils which relate to their use for commercial purposes,

(*b*) goods in transit other than passengers' baggage where the transit consists of or includes carriage by such ships or aircraft;

(2) Any liability, other than for bodily injury to passengers or loss of or damage to their baggage,

(*a*) arising out of the use or operation of ships, installations or aircraft as referred to in (1)(*a*) above in so far as the law of the Contracting State in which such aircraft are registered does not prohibit agreements on jurisdiction regarding insurance of such risks,

(*b*) for loss or damage caused by goods in transit as described in (1)(*b*) above;

(3) Any financial loss connected with the use or operation of ships, installations or aircraft as referred to in (1)(*a*) above, in particular loss of freight or charter-hire;

(4) Any risk or interest connected with any of those referred to in (1) to (3) above.

Section 4

Jurisdiction over consumer contracts

Article 13

In proceedings concerning a contract concluded by a person for a purpose which can be regarded as being outside his trade or profession, hereinafter called the "consumer", jurisdiction shall be determined by this Section, without prejudice to the provisions of Articles 4 and 5(5), if it is:

(1) a contract for the sale of goods on instalment credit terms, or

(2) a contract for a loan repayable by instalments, or for any other form of credit, made to finance the sale of goods, or

(3) any other contract for the supply of goods or a contract for the supply of services and

(*a*) in the State of the consumer's domicile the conclusion of the contract was preceded by a specific invitation addressed to him or by advertising, and

(*b*) the consumer took in that State the steps necessary for the conclusion of the contract.

Where a consumer enters into a contract with a party who is not domiciled in a Contracting State but has a branch, agency or other establishment in one of the Contracting States, that party shall, in disputes arising out of the operations of the branch, agency or establishment, be deemed to be domiciled in that State.

This Section shall not apply to contracts of transport.

Article 14

A consumer may bring proceedings against the other party to a contract either in the courts of the Contracting State in which that party is domiciled or in the courts of the Contracting State in which he is himself domiciled.

Proceedings may be brought against a consumer by the other party to the contract only in the courts of the Contracting State in which the consumer is domiciled.

SCH. 1

These provisions shall not affect the right to bring a counter-claim in the court in which, in accordance with this Section, the original claim is pending.

ARTICLE 15

The provisions of this Section may be departed from only by an agreement:

(1) which is entered into after the dispute has arisen, or

(2) which allows the consumer to bring proceedings in courts other than those indicated in this Section, or

(3) which is entered into by the consumer and the other party to the contract, both of whom are at the time of conclusion of the contract domiciled or habitually resident in the same Contracting State, and which confers jurisdiction on the courts of that State, provided that such an agreement is not contrary to the law of that State.

Section 5

Exclusive jurisdiction

ARTICLE 16

The following courts shall have exclusive jurisdiction, regardless of domicile:

(1) in proceedings which have as their object rights *in rem* in, or tenancies of, immovable property, the courts of the Contracting State in which the property is situated;

(2) in proceedings which have as their object the validity of the constitution, the nullity or the dissolution of companies or other legal persons or associations of natural or legal persons, or the decisions of their organs, the courts of the Contracting State in which the company, legal person or association has its seat;

(3) in proceedings which have as their object the validity of entries in public registers, the courts of the Contracting State in which the register is kept;

(4) in proceedings concerned with the registration or validity of patents, trade marks, designs, or other similar rights required to be deposited or registered, the courts of the Contracting State in which the deposit or registration has been applied for, has taken place or is under the terms of an international convention deemed to have taken place;

(5) in proceedings concerned with the enforcement of judgments, the courts of the Contracting State in which the judgment has been or is to be enforced. Sch. 1

Section 6

Prorogation of jurisdiction

Article 17

If the parties, one or more of whom is domiciled in a Contracting State, have agreed that a court or the courts of a Contracting State are to have jurisdiction to settle any disputes which have arisen or which may arise in connection with a particular legal relationship, that court or those courts shall have exclusive jurisdiction. Such an agreement conferring jurisdiction shall be either in writing or evidenced in writing or, in international trade or commerce, in a form which accords with practices in that trade or commerce of which the parties are or ought to have been aware. Where such an agreement is concluded by parties, none of whom is domiciled in a Contracting State, the courts of other Contracting States shall have no jurisdiction over their disputes unless the court or courts chosen have declined jurisdiction.

The court or courts of a Contracting State on which a trust instrument has conferred jurisdiction shall have exclusive jurisdiction in any proceedings brought against a settlor, trustee or beneficiary, if relations between these persons or their rights or obligations under the trust are involved.

Agreements or provisions of a trust instrument conferring jurisdiction shall have no legal force if they are contrary to the provisions of Articles 12 or 15, or if the courts whose jurisdiction they purport to exclude have exclusive jurisdiction by virtue of Article 16.

If an agreement conferring jurisdiction was concluded for the benefit of only one of the parties, that party shall retain the right to bring proceedings in any other court which has jurisdiction by virtue of this Convention.

Article 18

Apart from jurisdiction derived from other provisions of this Convention, a court of a Contracting State before whom a defendant enters an appearance shall have jurisdiction. This rule shall not apply where appearance was entered solely to contest the jurisdiction, or where another court has exclusive jurisdiction by virtue of Article 16.

SCH. 1

Section 7

Examination as to jurisdiction and admissibility

ARTICLE 19

Where a court of a Contracting State is seised of a claim which is principally concerned with a matter over which the courts of another Contracting State have exclusive jurisdiction by virtue of Article 16, it shall declare of its own motion that it has no jurisdiction.

ARTICLE 20

Where a defendant domiciled in one Contracting State is sued in a court of another Contracting State and does not enter an appearance, the court shall declare of its own motion that it has no jurisdiction unless its jurisdiction is derived from the provisions of this Convention.

The court shall stay the proceedings so long as it is not shown that the defendant has been able to receive the document instituting the proceedings or an equivalent document in sufficient time to enable him to arrange for his defence, or that all necessary steps have been taken to this end.

The provisions of the foregoing paragraph shall be replaced by those of Article 15 of the Hague Convention of 15 November 1965 on the Service Abroad of Judicial and Extrajudicial Documents in Civil or Commercial Matters, if the document instituting the proceedings or notice thereof had to be transmitted abroad in accordance with that Convention.

Section 8

Lis Pendens—Related actions

ARTICLE 21

Where proceedings involving the same cause of action and between the same parties are brought in the courts of different Contracting States, any court other than the court first seised shall of its own motion decline jurisdiction in favour of that court.

A court which would be required to decline jurisdiction may stay its proceedings if the jurisdiction of the other court is contested.

ARTICLE 22

Where related actions are brought in the courts of different Contracting States, any court other than the court first seised may, while the actions are pending at first instance, stay its proceedings.

A court other than the court first seised may also, on the application of one of the parties, decline jurisdiction if the law of that court permits the consolidation of related actions and the court first seised has jurisdiction over both actions.

For the purposes of this Article, actions are deemed to be related where they are so closely connected that it is expedient to hear and determine them together to avoid the risk of irreconcilable judgments resulting from separate proceedings.

Article 23

Where actions come within the exclusive jurisdiction of several courts, any court other than the court first seised shall decline jurisdiction in favour of that court.

Section 9

Provisional, including protective, measures

Article 24

Application may be made to the courts of a Contracting State for such provisional, including protective, measures as may be available under the law of that State, even if, under this Convention, the courts of another Contracting State have jurisdiction as to the substance of the matter.

TITLE III

RECOGNITION AND ENFORCEMENT

Article 25

For the purposes of this Convention, "judgment" means any judgment given by a court or tribunal of a Contracting State, whatever the judgment may be called, including a decree, order, decision or writ of execution, as well as the determination of costs or expenses by an officer of the court.

Section 1

Recognition

Article 26

A judgment given in a Contracting State shall be recognised in the other Contracting States without any special procedure being required.

Any interested party who raises the recognition of a judgment as the principal issue in a dispute may, in accordance with the procedures provided for in Sections 2 and 3 of this Title, apply for a decision that the judgment be recognised.

SCH. 1

If the outcome of proceedings in a court of a Contracting State depends on the determination of an incidental question of recognition that court shall have jurisdiction over that question.

ARTICLE 27

A judgment shall not be recognised:

(1) if such recognition is contrary to public policy in the State in which recognition is sought;

(2) where it was given in default of appearance, if the defendant was not duly served with the document which instituted the proceedings or with an equivalent document in sufficient time to enable him to arrange for his defence;

(3) if the judgment is irreconcilable with a judgment given in a dispute between the same parties in the State in which recognition is sought;

(4) if the court of the State in which the judgment was given, in order to arrive at its judgment, has decided a preliminary question concerning the status or legal capacity of natural persons, rights in property arising out of a matrimonial relationship, wills or succession in a way that conflicts with a rule of the private international law of the State in which the recognition is sought, unless the same result would have been reached by the application of the rules of private international law of that State;

(5) if the judgment is irreconcilable with an earlier judgment given in a non-Contracting State involving the same cause of action and between the same parties, provided that this latter judgment fulfils the conditions necessary for its recognition in the State addressed.

ARTICLE 28

Moreover, a judgment shall not be recognised if it conflicts with the provisions of Sections 3, 4 or 5 of Title II, or in a case provided for in Article 59.

In its examination of the grounds of jurisdiction referred to in the foregoing paragraph, the court or authority applied to shall be bound by the findings of fact on which the court of the State in which the judgment was given based its jurisdiction.

Subject to the provisions of the first paragraph, the jurisdiction of the court of the State in which the judgment was given may not be reviewed; the test of public policy referred to in Article 27(1) may not be applied to the rules relating to jurisdiction.

ARTICLE 29

Under no circumstances may a foreign judgment be reviewed as to its substance.

ARTICLE 30

A court of a Contracting State in which recognition is sought of a judgment given in another Contracting State may stay the proceedings if an ordinary appeal against the judgment has been lodged.

A court of a Contracting State in which recognition is sought of a judgment given in Ireland or the United Kingdom may stay the proceedings if enforcement is suspended in the State in which the judgment was given by reason of an appeal.

Section 2

Enforcement

ARTICLE 31

A judgment given in a Contracting State and enforceable in that State shall be enforced in another Contracting State when, on the application of any interested party, the order for its enforcement has been issued there.

However, in the United Kingdom, such a judgment shall be enforced in England and Wales, in Scotland, or in Northern Ireland when, on the application of any interested party, it has been registered for enforcement in that part of the United Kingdom.

ARTICLE 32

The application shall be submitted:

— in Belgium, to the *tribunal de première instance* or *rechtbank van eerste aanleg ;*

— in Denmark, to the *underret ;*

— in the Federal Republic of Germany, to the presiding judge of a chamber of the *Landgericht ;*

— in France, to the presiding judge of the *tribunal de grande instance ;*

— in Ireland, to the High Court ;

— in Italy, to the *corte d'appello ;*

— in Luxembourg, to the presiding judge of the *tribunal d'arrondissement ;*

— in the Netherlands, to the presiding judge of the *arrondissementsrechtbank ;*

— in the United Kingdom:

SCH. 1

(1) in England and Wales, to the High Court of Justice, or in the case of a maintenance judgment to the Magistrates' Court on transmission by the Secretary of State ;

(2) in Scotland, to the Court of Session, or in the case of a maintenance judgment to the Sheriff Court on transmission by the Secretary of State ;

(3) in Northern Ireland, to the High Court of Justice, or in the case of a maintenance judgment to the Magistrates' Court on transmission by the Secretary of State.

The jurisdiction of local courts shall be determined by reference to the place of domicile of the party against whom enforcement is sought. If he is not domiciled in the State in which enforcement is sought, it shall be determined by reference to the place of enforcement.

ARTICLE 33

The procedure for making the application shall be governed by the law of the State in which enforcement is sought.

The applicant must give an address for service of process within the area of jurisdiction of the court applied to. However, if the law of the State in which enforcement is sought does not provide for the furnishing of such an address, the applicant shall appoint a representative *ad litem*.

The documents referred to in Articles 46 and 47 shall be attached to the application.

ARTICLE 34

The court applied to shall give its decision without delay ; the party against whom enforcement is sought shall not at this stage of the proceedings be entitled to make any submissions on the application.

The application may be refused only for one of the reasons specified in Articles 27 and 28.

Under no circumstances may the foreign judgment be reviewed as to its substance.

ARTICLE 35

The appropriate officer of the court shall without delay bring the decision given on the application to the notice of the applicant in accordance with the procedure laid down by the law of the State in which enforcement is sought.

ARTICLE 36

If enforcement is authorised, the party against whom enforcement is sought may appeal against the decision within one month of service thereof.

If that party is domiciled in a Contracting State other than that in which the decision authorising enforcement was given, the time for appealing shall be two months and shall run from the date of service, either on him in person or at his residence. No extension of time may be granted on account of distance.

Article 37

An appeal against the decision authorising enforcement shall be lodged in accordance with the rules governing procedure in contentious matters:

— in Belgium, with the *tribunal de première instance* or *rechtbank van eerste aanleg;*

— in Denmark, with the *landsret;*

— in the Federal Republic of Germany, with the *Oberlandesgericht;*

— in France, with the *cour d'appel;*

— in Ireland, with the High Court;

— in Italy, with the *corte d'appello;*

— in Luxembourg, with the *Cour supérieure de Justice* sitting as a court of civil appeal;

— in the Netherlands, with the *arrondissementsrechtbank;*

— in the United Kingdom:

(1) in England and Wales, with the High Court of Justice, or in the case of a maintenance judgment with the Magistrates' Court;

(2) in Scotland, with the Court of Session, or in the case of a maintenance judgment with the Sheriff Court;

(3) in Northern Ireland, with the High Court of Justice, or in the case of a maintenance judgment with the Magistrates' Court.

The judgment given on the appeal may be contested only:

— in Belgium, France, Italy, Luxembourg and the Netherlands, by an appeal in cassation;

— in Denmark, by an appeal to the *højesteret,* with the leave of the Minister of Justice;

— in the Federal Republic of Germany, by a *Rechtsbeschwerde;*

— in Ireland, by an appeal on a point of law to the Supreme Court;

— in the United Kingdom, by a single further appeal on a point of law.

SCH. 1

ARTICLE 38

The court with which the appeal under the first paragraph of Article 37 is lodged may, on the application of the appellant, stay the proceedings if an ordinary appeal has been lodged against the judgment in the State in which that judgment was given or if the time for such an appeal has not yet expired ; in the latter case, the court may specify the time within which such an appeal is to be lodged.

Where the judgment was given in Ireland or the United Kingdom, any form of appeal available in the State in which it was given shall be treated as an ordinary appeal for the purposes of the first paragraph.

The court may also make enforcement conditional on the provision of such security as it shall determine.

ARTICLE 39

During the time specified for an appeal pursuant to Article 36 and until any such appeal has been determined, no measures of enforcement may be taken other than protective measures taken against the property of the party against whom enforcement is sought.

The decision authorising enforcement shall carry with it the power to proceed to any such protective measures.

ARTICLE 40

If the application for enforcement is refused, the applicant may appeal:

— in Belgium, to the *cour d'appel* or *hof van beroep ;*

— in Denmark, to the *landsret ;*

— in the Federal Republic of Germany, to the *Oberlandesgericht ;*

— in France, to the *cour d'appel ;*

— in Ireland, to the High Court ;

— in Italy, to the *corte d'appello* ;

— in Luxembourg, to the *Cour supérieure de Justice* sitting as a court of civil appeal ;

— in the Netherlands, to the *gerechtshof ;*

— in the United Kingdom:

(1) in England and Wales, to the High Court of Justice, or in the case of a maintenance judgment to the Magistrates' Court ;

(2) in Scotland, to the Court of Session, or in the case of a maintenance judgment to the Sheriff Court ;

(3) in Northern Ireland, to the High Court of Justice, or in the case of a maintenance judgment to the Magistrates' Court. Sch. 1

The party against whom enforcement is sought shall be summoned to appear before the appellate court. If he fails to appear, the provisions of the second and third paragraphs of Article 20 shall apply even where he is not domiciled in any of the Contracting States.

ARTICLE 41

A judgment given on an appeal provided for in Article 40 may be contested only:

— in Belgium, France, Italy, Luxembourg and the Netherlands, by an appeal in cassation ;

— in Denmark, by an appeal to the *højesteret,* with the leave of the Minister of Justice ;

— in the Federal Republic of Germany, by a *Rechtsbeschwerde ;*

— in Ireland, by an appeal on a point of law to the Supreme Court ;

— in the United Kingdom, by a single further appeal on a point of law.

ARTICLE 42

Where a foreign judgment has been given in respect of several matters and enforcement cannot be authorised for all of them, the court shall authorise enforcement for one or more of them.

An applicant may request partial enforcement of a judgment.

ARTICLE 43

A foreign judgment which orders a periodic payment by way of a penalty shall be enforceable in the State in which enforcement is sought only if the amount of the payment has been finally determined by the courts of the State in which the judgment was given.

ARTICLE 44

An applicant who, in the State in which the judgment was given, has benefited from complete or partial legal aid or exemption from costs or expenses, shall be entitled, in the procedures provided for in Articles 32 to 35, to benefit from the most favourable legal aid or the most extensive exemption from costs or expenses provided for by the law of the State addressed.

An applicant who requests the enforcement of a decision given by an administrative authority in Denmark in respect of a

SCH. 1 maintenance order may, in the State addressed, claim the benefits referred to in the first paragraph if he presents a statement from the Danish Ministry of Justice to the effect that he fulfils the economic requirements to qualify for the grant of complete or partial legal aid or exemption from costs or expenses.

ARTICLE 45

No security, bond or deposit, however described, shall be required of a party who in one Contracting State applies for enforcement of a judgment given in another Contracting State on the ground that he is a foreign national or that he is not domiciled or resident in the State in which enforcement is sought.

Section 3

Common provisions

ARTICLE 46

A party seeking recognition or applying for enforcement of a judgment shall produce:

(1) a copy of the judgment which satisfies the conditions necessary to establish its authenticity;

(2) in the case of a judgment given in default, the original or a certified true copy of the document which establishes that the party in default was served with the document instituting the proceedings or with an equivalent document.

ARTICLE 47

A party applying for enforcement shall also produce:

(1) documents which establish that, according to the law of the State in which it has been given, the judgment is enforceable and has been served;

(2) where appropriate, a document showing that the applicant is in receipt of legal aid in the State in which the judgment was given.

ARTICLE 48

If the documents specified in Article 46(2) and Article 47(2) are not produced, the court may specify a time for their production, accept equivalent documents or, if it considers that it has sufficient information before it, dispense with their production.

If the court so requires, a translation of the documents shall be produced; the translation shall be certified by a person qualified to do so in one of the Contracting States.

ARTICLE 49

No legalisation or other similar formality shall be required in respect of the documents referred to in Articles 46 or 47 or the second paragraph of Article 48, or in respect of a document appointing a representative *ad litem*.

TITLE IV

AUTHENTIC INSTRUMENTS AND COURT SETTLEMENTS

Article 50

A document which has been formally drawn up or registered as an authentic instrument and is enforceable in one Contracting State shall, in another Contracting State, have an order for its enforcement issued there, on application made in accordance with the procedures provided for in Article 31 *et seq*. The application may be refused only if enforcement of the instrument is contrary to public policy in the State in which enforcement is sought.

The instrument produced must satisfy the conditions necessary to establish its authenticity in the State of origin.

The provisions of Section 3 of Title III shall apply as appropriate.

Article 51

A settlement which has been approved by a court in the course of proceedings and is enforceable in the State in which it was concluded shall be enforceable in the State in which enforcement is sought under the same conditions as authentic instruments.

TITLE V

GENERAL PROVISIONS

Article 52

In order to determine whether a party is domiciled in the Contracting State whose courts are seised of the matter, the court shall apply its internal law.

If a party is not domiciled in the State whose courts are seised of the matter, then, in order to determine whether the party is domiciled in another Contracting State, the court shall apply the law of that State.

The domicile of a party shall, however, be determined in accordance with his national law if, by that law, his domicile depends on that of another person or on the seat of an authority.

Article 53

For the purposes of this Convention, the seat of a company or other legal person or association of natural or legal persons shall be treated as its domicile. However, in order to determine that seat, the court shall apply its rules of private international law.

In order to determine whether a trust is domiciled in the Contracting State whose courts are seised of the matter, the court shall apply its rules of private international law.

SCH. 1

TITLE VI

TRANSITIONAL PROVISIONS

ARTICLE 54

The provisions of this Convention shall apply only to legal proceedings instituted and to documents formally drawn up or registered as authentic instruments after its entry into force.

However, judgments given after the date of entry into force of this Convention in proceedings instituted before that date shall be recognised and enforced in accordance with the provisions of Title III if jurisdiction was founded upon rules which accorded with those provided for either in Title II of this Convention or in a convention concluded between the State of origin and the State addressed which was in force when the proceedings were instituted.

TITLE VII

RELATIONSHIP TO OTHER CONVENTIONS

ARTICLE 55

Subject to the provisions of the second paragraph of Article 54, and of Article 56, this Convention shall, for the States which are parties to it, supersede the following conventions concluded between two or more of them:

— the Convention between Belgium and France on Jurisdiction and the Validity and Enforcement of Judgments, Arbitration Awards and Authentic Instruments, signed at Paris on 8 July 1899;

— the Convention between Belgium and the Netherlands on Jurisdiction, Bankruptcy, and the Validity and Enforcement of Judgments, Arbitration Awards and Authentic Instruments, signed at Brussels on 28 March 1925;

— the Convention between France and Italy on the Enforcement of Judgments in Civil and Commercial Matters, signed at Rome on 3 June 1930;

— the Convention between the United Kingdom and the French Republic providing for the Reciprocal Enforcement of Judgments in Civil and Commercial Matters, with Protocol, signed at Paris on 18 January 1934;

— the Convention between the United Kingdom and the Kingdom of Belgium providing for the Reciprocal Enforcement of Judgments in Civil and Commercial Matters, with Protocol, signed at Brussels on 2 May 1934;

—the Convention between Germany and Italy on the Recognition and Enforcement of Judgments in Civil and Commercial matters, signed at Rome on 9 March 1936;

— the Convention between the Federal Republic of Germany and the Kingdom of Belgium on the Mutual Recognition and Enforcement of Judgments, Arbitration Awards and Authentic Instruments in Civil and Commercial Matters, signed at Bonn on 30 June 1958 ;

— the Convention between the Kingdom of the Netherlands and the Italian Republic on the Recognition and Enforcement of Judgments in Civil and Commercial Matters, signed at Rome on 17 April 1959 ;

— the Convention between the United Kingdom and the Federal Republic of Germany for the Reciprocal Recognition and Enforcement of Judgments in Civil and Commercial Matters, signed at Bonn on 14 July 1960 ;

— the Convention between the Kingdom of Belgium and the Italian Republic on the Recognition and Enforcement of Judgments and other Enforceable Instruments in Civil and Commercial Matters, signed at Rome on 6 April 1962 ;

— the Convention between the Kingdom of the Netherlands and the Federal Republic of Germany on the Mutual Recognition and Enforcement of Judgments and other Enforceable Instruments in Civil and Commercial Matters, signed at The Hague on 30 August 1962 ;

— the Convention between the United Kingdom and the Republic of Italy for the Reciprocal Recognition and Enforcement of Judgments in Civil and Commercial Matters, signed at Rome on 7 February 1964, with amending Protocol signed at Rome on 14 July 1970 ;

— the Convention between the United Kingdom and the Kingdom of the Netherlands providing for the Reciprocal Recognition and Enforcement of Judgments in Civil Matters, signed at The Hague on 17 November 1967,

and, in so far as it is in force:

— the Treaty between Belgium, the Netherlands and Luxembourg on Jurisdiction, Bankruptcy, and the Validity and Enforcement of Judgments, Arbitration Awards and Authentic Instruments, signed at Brussels on 24 November 1961.

ARTICLE 56

The Treaty and the conventions referred to in Article 55 shall continue to have effect in relation to matters to which this Convention does not apply.

They shall continue to have effect in respect of judgments given and documents formally drawn up or registered as authentic instruments before the entry into force of this Convention.

SCH. 1

ARTICLE 57

This Convention shall not affect any conventions to which the Contracting States are or will be parties and which, in relation to particular matters, govern jurisdiction or the recognition or enforcement of judgments.

This Convention shall not affect the application of provisions which, in relation to particular matters, govern jurisdiction or the recognition or enforcement of judgments and which are or will be contained in acts of the Institutions of the European Communities or in national laws harmonised in implementation of such acts.

(*Article* 25(2) *of the Accession Convention provides:*

" With a view to its uniform interpretation, paragraph 1 of Article 57 shall be applied in the following manner:

(*a*) The 1968 Convention as amended shall not prevent a court of a Contracting State which is a party to a convention on a particular matter from assuming jurisdiction in accordance with that convention, even where the defendant is domiciled in another Contracting State which is not a party to that convention. The court shall, in any event, apply Article 20 of the 1968 Convention as amended.

(*b*) A judgment given in a Contracting State in the exercise of jurisdiction provided for in a convention on a particular matter shall be recognised and enforced in the other Contracting States in accordance with the 1968 Convention as amended.

Where a convention on a particular matter to which both the State of origin and the State addressed are parties lays down conditions for the recognition or enforcement of judgments, those conditions shall apply. In any event, the provisions of the 1968 Convention as amended which concern the procedures for recognition and enforcement of judgments may be applied.")

ARTICLE 58

This Convention shall not affect the rights granted to Swiss nationals by the Convention concluded on 15 June 1869 between France and the Swiss Confederation on Jurisdiction and the Enforcement of Judgments in Civil Matters.

ARTICLE 59

This Convention shall not prevent a Contracting State from assuming, in a convention on the recognition and enforcement of judgments, an obligation towards a third State not to recognise judgments given in other Contracting States against defendants domiciled or habitually resident in the third State where, in cases provided for in Article 4, the judgment could only be founded on a ground of jurisdiction specified in the second paragraph of Article 3.

However, a Contracting State may not assume an obligation towards a third State not to recognise a judgment given in another Contracting State by a court basing its jurisdiction on the presence within that State of property belonging to the defendant, or the seizure by the plaintiff of property situated there:

(1) if the action is brought to assert or declare proprietary or possessory rights in that property, seeks to obtain authority to dispose of it, or arises from another issue relating to such property, or,

(2) if the property constitutes the security for a debt which is the subject-matter of the action.

TITLE VIII

FINAL PROVISIONS

Article 60

This Convention shall apply to the European territories of the Contracting States, including Greenland, to the French overseas departments and territories, and to Mayotte.

The Kingdom of the Netherlands may declare at the time of signing or ratifying this Convention or at any later time, by notifying the Secretary-General of the Council of the European Communities, that this Convention shall be applicable to the Netherlands Antilles. In the absence of such declaration, proceedings taking place in the European territory of the Kingdom as a result of an appeal in cassation from the judgment of a court in the Netherlands Antilles shall be deemed to be proceedings taking place in the latter court.

Notwithstanding the first paragraph, this Convention shall not apply to:

(1) the Faroe Islands, unless the Kingdom of Denmark makes a declaration to the contrary,

(2) any European territory situated outside the United Kingdom for the international relations of which the United Kingdom is responsible, unless the United Kingdom makes a declaration to the contrary in respect of any such territory.

Such declarations may be made at any time by notifying the Secretary-General of the Council of the European Communities.

Proceedings brought in the United Kingdom on appeal from courts in one of the territories referred to in subparagraph (2) of the third paragraph shall be deemed to be proceedings taking place in those courts.

Proceedings which in the Kingdom of Denmark are dealt with under the law on civil procedure for the Faroe Islands (*lov for Faerøerne om rettens pleje*) shall be deemed to be proceedings taking place in the courts of the Faroe Islands.

Sch. 1

Article 61

This Convention shall be ratified by the signatory States. The instruments of ratification shall be deposited with the Secretary-General of the Council of the European Communities.

Article 62

This Convention shall enter into force on the first day of the third month following the deposit of the instrument of ratification by the last signatory State to take this step.

Article 63

The Contracting States recognise that any State which becomes a member of the European Economic Community shall be required to accept this Convention as a basis for the negotiations between the Contracting States and that State necessary to ensure the implementation of the last paragraph of Article 220 of the Treaty establishing the European Economic Community.

The necessary adjustments may be the subject of a special convention between the Contracting States of the one part and the new Member State of the other part.

Article 64

The Secretary-General of the Council of the European Communities shall notify the signatory States of:

(*a*) the deposit of each instrument of ratification ;

(*b*) the date of entry into force of this Convention ;

(*c*) any declaration received pursuant to Article 60 ;

(*d*) any declaration received pursuant to Article IV of the Protocol ;

(*e*) any communication made pursuant to Article VI of the Protocol.

Article 65

The Protocol annexed to this Convention by common accord of the Contracting States shall form an integral part thereof.

Article 66

This Convention is concluded for an unlimited period.

Article 67

Any Contracting State may request the revision of this Convention. In this event, a revision conference shall be convened by the President of the Council of the European Communities.

Article 68

This Convention, drawn up in a single original in the Dutch, French, German and Italian languages, all four texts being equally authentic, shall be deposited in the archives of the

Secretariat of the Council of the European Communities. The Secretary-General shall transmit a certified copy to the Government of each signatory State.

(Signatures of Plenipotentiaries of the original six Contracting States)

ANNEXED PROTOCOL

Article I

Any person domiciled in Luxembourg who is sued in a court of another Contracting State pursuant to Article 5(1) may refuse to submit to the jurisdiction of that court. If the defendant does not enter an appearance the court shall declare of its own motion that it has no jurisdiction.

An agreement conferring jurisdiction, within the meaning of Article 17, shall be valid with respect to a person domiciled in Luxembourg only if that person has expressly and specifically so agreed.

Article II

Without prejudice to any more favourable provisions of national laws, persons domiciled in a Contracting State who are being prosecuted in the criminal courts of another Contracting State of which they are not nationals for an offence which was not intentionally committed may be defended by persons qualified to do so, even if they do not appear in person.

However, the court seised of the matter may order appearance in person ; in the case of failure to appear, a judgment given in the civil action without the person concerned having had the opportunity to arrange for his defence need not be recognised or enforced in the other Contracting States.

Article III

In proceedings for the issue of an order for enforcement, no charge, duty or fee calculated by reference to the value of the matter in issue may be levied in the State in which enforcement is sought.

Article IV

Judicial and extrajudicial documents drawn up in one Contracting State which have to be served on persons in another Contracting State shall be transmitted in accordance with the procedures laid down in the conventions and agreements concluded between the Contracting States.

Unless the State in which service is to take place objects by declaration to the Secretary-General of the Council of the European Communities, such documents may also be sent by the appropriate public officers of the State in which the document has been drawn up directly to the appropriate public officers

SCH. 1

of the State in which the addressee is to be found. In this case the officer of the State of origin shall send a copy of the document to the officer of the State addressed who is competent to forward it to the addressee. The document shall be forwarded in the manner specified by the law of the State addressed. The forwarding shall be recorded by a certificate sent directly to the officer of the State of origin.

ARTICLE V

The jurisdiction specified in Article 6(2) and Article 10 in actions on a warranty or guarantee or in any other third party proceedings may not be resorted to in the Federal Republic of Germany. In that State, any person domiciled in another Contracting State may be sued in the courts in pursuance of Articles 68, 72, 73 and 74 of the code of civil procedure (*Zivilprozessordnung*) concerning third-party notices.

Judgments given in the other Contracting States by virtue of Article 6(2) or Article 10 shall be recognised and enforced in the Federal Republic of Germany in accordance with Title III. Any effects which judgments given in that State may have on third parties by application of Articles 68, 72, 73 and 74 of the code of civil procedure (*Zivilprozessordnung*) shall also be recognised in the other Contracting States.

ARTICLE V A

In matters relating to maintenance, the expression " court " includes the Danish administrative authorities.

ARTICLE V B

In proceedings involving a dispute between the master and a member of the crew of a sea-going ship registered in Denmark or in Ireland, concerning remuneration or other conditions of service, a court in a Contracting State shall establish whether the diplomatic or consular officer responsible for the ship has been notified of the dispute. It shall stay the proceedings so long as he has not been notified. It shall of its own motion decline jurisdiction if the officer, having been duly notified, has exercised the powers accorded to him in the matter by a consular convention, or in the absence of such a convention, has, within the time allowed, raised any objection to the exercise of such jurisdiction.

ARTICLE V C

Articles 52 and 53 of this Convention shall, when applied by Article 69(5) of the Convention for the European Patent for the Common Market, signed at Luxembourg on 15 December 1975, to the provisions relating to " residence " in the English text of that Convention, operate as if " residence " in that text were the same as " domicile " in Articles 52 and 53.

Sch. 1

Article V D

Without prejudice to the jurisdiction of the European Patent Office under the Convention on the Grant of European Patents, signed at Munich on 5 October 1973, the courts of each Contracting State shall have exclusive jurisdiction, regardless of domicile, in proceedings concerned with the registration or validity of any European patent granted for that State which is not a Community patent by virtue of the provisions of Article 86 of the Convention for the European Patent for the Common Market, signed at Luxembourg on 15 December 1975.

Article VI

The Contracting States shall communicate to the Secretary-General of the Council of the European Communities the text of any provisions of their laws which amend either those articles of their laws mentioned in the Convention or the lists of courts specified in Section 2 of Title III of the Convention.

SCHEDULE 2

Section 2(2).

Text of 1971 Protocol, as Amended

Article 1

The Court of Justice of the European Communities shall have jurisdiction to give rulings on the interpretation of the Convention on Jurisdiction and the Enforcement of Judgments in Civil and Commercial Matters and of the Protocol annexed to that Convention, signed at Brussels on 27 September 1968, and also on the interpretation of the present Protocol.

The Court of Justice of the European Communities shall also have jurisdiction to give rulings on the interpretation of the Convention on the Accession of the Kingdom of Denmark, Ireland and the United Kingdom of Great Britain and Northern Ireland to the Convention of 27 September 1968 and to this Protocol.

Article 2

The following courts may request the Court of Justice to give preliminary rulings on questions of interpretation:

(1) — in Belgium: *la Cour de Cassation—het Hof van Cassatie* and *le Conseil d'Etat—de Raad van State,*

— in Denmark: *højesteret,*

— in the Federal Republic of Germany: *die obersten Gerichtshöfe des Bundes,*

— in France: *la Cour de Cassation* and *le Conseil d'Etat,*

— in Ireland: the Supreme Court,

— in Italy: *la Corte Suprema di Cassazione,*

SCH. 2

— in Luxembourg: *la Cour supérieure de Justice* when sitting as *Cour de Cassation,*

— in the Netherlands: *de Hoge Raad,*

— in the United Kingdom: the House of Lords and courts to which application has been made under the second paragraph of Article 37 or under Article 41 of the Convention;

(2) the courts of the Contracting States when they are sitting in an appellate capacity;

(3) in the cases provided for in Article 37 of the Convention, the courts referred to in that Article.

ARTICLE 3

(1) Where a question of interpretation of the Convention or of one of the other instruments referred to in Article 1 is raised in a case pending before one of the courts listed in Article 2(1), that court shall, if it considers that a decision on the question is necessary to enable it to give judgment, request the Court of Justice to give a ruling thereon.

(2) Where such a question is raised before any court referred to in Article 2(2) or (3), that court may, under the conditions laid down in paragraph (1), request the Court of Justice to give a ruling thereon.

ARTICLE 4

(1) The competent authority of a Contracting State may request the Court of Justice to give a ruling on a question of interpretation of the Convention or of one of the other instruments referred to in Article 1 if judgments given by courts of that State conflict with the interpretation given either by the Court of Justice or in a judgment of one of the courts of another Contracting State referred to in Article 2(1) or (2). The provisions of this paragraph shall apply only to judgments which have become *res judicata.*

(2) The interpretation given by the Court of Justice in response to such a request shall not affect the judgments which gave rise to the request for interpretation.

(3) The Procurators-General of the Courts of Cassation of the Contracting States, or any other authority designated by a Contracting State, shall be entitled to request the Court of Justice for a ruling on interpretation in accordance with paragraph (1).

(4) The Registrar of the Court of Justice shall give notice of the request to the Contracting States, to the Commission and to the Council of the European Communities; they shall then be entitled within two months of the notification to submit statements of case or written observations to the Court.

(5) No fees shall be levied or any costs or expenses awarded in respect of the proceedings provided for in this Article. **Sch. 2**

Article 5

(1) Except where this Protocol otherwise provides, the provisions of the Treaty establishing the European Economic Community and those of the Protocol on the Statute of the Court of Justice annexed thereto, which are applicable when the Court is requested to give a preliminary ruling, shall also apply to any proceedings for the interpretation of the Convention and the other instruments referred to in Article 1.

(2) The Rules of Procedure of the Court of Justice shall, if necessary, be adjusted and supplemented in accordance with Article 188 of the Treaty establishing the European Economic Community.

Article 6

This Protocol shall apply to the European territories of the Contracting States, including Greenland, to the French overseas departments and territories, and to Mayotte.

The Kingdom of the Netherlands may declare at the time of signing or ratifying this Protocol or at any later time, by notifying the Secretary-General of the Council of the European Communities, that this Protocol shall be applicable to the Netherlands Antilles.

Notwithstanding the first paragraph, this Protocol shall not apply to:

(1) the Faroe Islands, unless the Kingdom of Denmark makes a declaration to the contrary,

(2) any European territory situated outside the United Kingdom for the international relations of which the United Kingdom is responsible, unless the United Kingdom makes a declaration to the contrary in respect of any such territory.

Such declarations may be made at any time by notifying the Secretary-General of the Council of the European Communities.

Article 7

This Protocol shall be ratified by the signatory States. The instruments of ratification shall be deposited with the Secretary-General of the Council of the European Communities.

Article 8

This Protocol shall enter into force on the first day of the third month following the deposit of the instrument of ratification by the last signatory State to take this step; provided that

SCH. 2

it shall at the earliest enter into force at the same time as the Convention of 27 September 1968 on Jurisdiction and the Enforcement of Judgments in Civil and Commercial Matters.

ARTICLE 9

The Contracting States recognise that any State which becomes a member of the European Economic Community, and to which Article 63 of the Convention on Jurisdiction and the Enforcement of Judgments in Civil and Commercial Matters applies, must accept the provisions of this Protocol, subject to such adjustments as may be required.

ARTICLE 10

The Secretary-General of the Council of the European Communities shall notify the signatory States of:

(*a*) the deposit of each instrument of ratification ;

(*b*) the date of entry into force of this Protocol ;

(*c*) any designation received pursuant to Article 4(3) ;

(*d*) any declaration received pursuant to Article 6.

ARTICLE 11

The Contracting States shall communicate to the Secretary-General of the Council of the European Communities the texts of any provisions of their laws which necessitate an amendment to the list of courts in Article 2(1).

ARTICLE 12

This Protocol is concluded for an unlimited period.

ARTICLE 13

Any Contracting State may request the revision of this Protocol. In this event, a revision conference shall be convened by the President of the Council of the European Communities.

ARTICLE 14

This Protocol, drawn up in a single original in the Dutch, French, German and Italian languages, all four texts being equally authentic, shall be deposited in the archives of the Secretariat of the Council of the European Communities. The Secretary-General shall transmit a certified copy to the Government of each signatory State.

SCHEDULE 3

Section 2(2).

Text of Titles V and VI of Accession Convention

TITLE V

TRANSITIONAL PROVISIONS

Article 34

(1) The 1968 Convention and the 1971 Protocol, with the amendments made by this Convention, shall apply only to legal proceedings instituted and to authentic instruments formally drawn up or registered after the entry into force of this Convention in the State of origin and, where recognition or enforcement of a judgment or authentic instrument is sought, in the State addressed.

(2) However, as between the six Contracting States to the 1968 Convention, judgments given after the date of entry into force of this Convention in proceedings instituted before that date shall be recognised and enforced in accordance with the provisions of Title III of the 1968 Convention as amended.

(3) Moreover, as between the six Contracting States to the 1968 Convention and the three States mentioned in Article 1 of this Convention, and as between those three States, judgments given after the date of entry into force of this Convention between the State of origin and the State addressed in proceedings instituted before that date shall also be recognised and enforced in accordance with the provisions of Title III of the 1968 Convention as amended if jurisdiction was founded upon rules which accorded with the provisions of Title II, as amended, or with provisions of a convention concluded between the State of origin and the State addressed which was in force when the proceedings were instituted.

Article 35

If the parties to a dispute concerning a contract had agreed in writing before the entry into force of this Convention that the contract was to be governed by the law of Ireland or of a part of the United Kingdom, the courts of Ireland or of that part of the United Kingdom shall retain the right to exercise jurisdiction in the dispute.

Article 36

For a period of three years from the entry into force of the 1968 Convention for the Kingdom of Denmark and Ireland respectively, jurisdiction in maritime matters shall be determined in these States not only in accordance with the provisions of that

SCH. 3

Convention but also in accordance with the provisions of paragraphs (1) to (6) following. However, upon the entry into force of the International Convention relating to the Arrest of Sea-going Ships, signed at Brussels on 10 May 1952, for one of these States, these provisions shall cease to have effect for that State.

(1) A person who is domiciled in a Contracting State may be sued in the courts of one of the States mentioned above in respect of a maritime claim if the ship to which the claim relates or any other ship owned by him has been arrested by judicial process within the territory of the latter State to secure the claim, or could have been so arrested there but bail or other security has been given, and either:

(*a*) the claimant is domiciled in the latter State; or

(*b*) the claim arose in the latter State; or

(*c*) the claim concerns the voyage during which the arrest was made or could have been made; or

(*d*) the claim arises out of a collision or out of damage caused by a ship to another ship or to goods or persons on board either ship, either by the execution or non-execution of a manoeuvre or by the non-observance of regulations; or

(*e*) the claim is for salvage; or

(*f*) the claim is in respect of a mortgage or hypothecation of the ship arrested.

(2) A claimant may arrest either the particular ship to which the maritime claim relates, or any other ship which is owned by the person who was, at the time when the maritime claim arose, the owner of the particular ship. However, only the particular ship to which the maritime claim relates may be arrested in respect of the maritime claims set out in subparagraphs (*o*), (*p*) or (*q*) of paragraph (5) of this Article.

(3) Ships shall be deemed to be in the same ownership when all the shares therein are owned by the same person or persons.

(4) When in the case of a charter by demise of a ship the charterer alone is liable in respect of a maritime claim relating to that ship, the claimant may arrest that ship or any other ship owned by the charterer, but no other ship owned by the owner may be arrested in respect of such claim. The same shall apply to any case in which a person other than the owner of a ship is liable in respect of a maritime claim relating to that ship.

(5) The expression " maritime claim " means a claim arising out of one or more of the following:

(*a*) damage caused by any ship either in collision or otherwise;

(*b*) loss of life or personal injury caused by any ship or occurring in connection with the operation of any ship;

(*c*) salvage;

(*d*) agreement relating to the use or hire of any ship whether by charterparty or otherwise;

(*e*) agreement relating to the carriage of goods in any ship whether by charterparty or otherwise;

(*f*) loss of or damage to goods including baggage carried in any ship;

(*g*) general average;

(*h*) bottomry;

(*i*) towage;

(*j*) pilotage;

(*k*) goods or materials wherever supplied to a ship for her operation or maintenance;

(*l*) construction, repair or equipment of any ship or dock charges and dues;

(*m*) wages of masters, officers or crew;

(*n*) master's disbursements, including disbursements made by shippers, charterers or agents on behalf of a ship or her owner;

(*o*) dispute as to the title to or ownership of any ship;

(*p*) disputes between co-owners of any ship as to the ownership, possession, employment or earnings of that ship;

(*q*) the mortgage or hypothecation of any ship.

(6) In Denmark, the expression " arrest " shall be deemed as regards the maritime claims referred to in subparagraphs (*o*) and (*p*) of paragraph (5) of this Article, to include a *forbud*, where that is the only procedure allowed in respect of such a claim under Articles 646 to 653 of the law on civil procedure (*lov om rettens pleje*).

TITLE VI

FINAL PROVISIONS

Article 37

The Secretary-General of the Council of the European Communities shall transmit a certified copy of the 1968 Convention and of the 1971 Protocol in the Dutch, French, German and Italian languages to the Governments of the Kingdom of Denmark, Ireland and the United Kingdom of Great Britain and Northern Ireland.

SCH. 3

The texts of the 1968 Convention and the 1971 Protocol, drawn up in the Danish, English and Irish languages, shall be annexed to this Convention. The texts drawn up in the Danish, English and Irish languages shall be authentic under the same conditions as the original texts of the 1968 Convention and the 1971 Protocol.

ARTICLE 38

This Convention shall be ratified by the signatory States. The instruments of ratification shall be deposited with the Secretary-General of the Council of the European Communities.

ARTICLE 39

This Convention shall enter into force, as between the States which shall have ratified it, on the first day of the third month following the deposit of the last instrument of ratification by the original Member States of the Community and one new Member State.

It shall enter into force for each new Member State which subsequently ratifies it on the first day of the third month following the deposit of its instrument of ratification.

ARTICLE 40

The Secretary-General of the Council of the European Communities shall notify the signatory States of:

(*a*) the deposit of each instrument of ratification,

(*b*) the dates of entry into force of this Convention for the Contracting States.

ARTICLE 41

This Convention, drawn up in a single original in the Danish, Dutch, English, French, German, Irish and Italian languages, all seven texts being equally authentic, shall be deposited in the archives of the Secretariat of the Council of the European Communities. The Secretary-General shall transmit a certified copy to the Government of each signatory State.

SCHEDULE 4

Section 16

Title II of 1968 Convention as Modified for Allocation of Jurisdiction Within U.K.

TITLE II

JURISDICTION

Section 1

General Provisions

Article 2

Subject to the provisions of this **Title,** persons domiciled in a **part of the United Kingdom** shall . . . be sued in the courts of that **part.**

. . . .

Article 3

Persons domiciled in a **part of the United Kingdom** may be sued in the courts of another **part of the United Kingdom** only by virtue of the rules set out in Sections 2, **4, 5 and** 6 of this Title.

. . . .

Section 2

Special jurisdiction

Article 5

A person domiciled in a **part of the United Kingdom** may, in another **part of the United Kingdom,** be sued:

(1) in matters relating to a contract, in the courts for the place of performance of the obligation in question ;

(2) in matters relating to maintenance, in the courts for the place where the maintenance creditor is domiciled or habitually resident or, if the matter is ancillary to proceedings concerning the status of a person, in the court which, according to its own law, has jurisdiction to entertain those proceedings, unless that jurisdiction is based solely on the nationality of one of the parties ;

(3) in matters relating to tort, delict or quasi-delict, in the courts for the place where the harmful event occurred **or in the case of a threatened wrong is likely to occur** ;

SCH. 4

(4) as regards a civil claim for damages or restitution which is based on an act giving rise to criminal proceedings, in the court seised of those proceedings, to the extent that that court has jurisdiction under its own law to entertain civil proceedings ;

(5) as regards a dispute arising out of the operations of a branch, agency or other establishment, in the courts for the place in which the branch, agency or other establishment is situated ;

(6) in his capacity as a settlor, trustee or beneficiary of a trust created by the operation of a statute, or by a written instrument, or created orally and evidenced in writing, in the courts of the **part of the United Kingdom** in which the trust is domiciled ;

(7) as regards a dispute concerning the payment of remuneration claimed in respect of the salvage of a cargo or freight, in the court under the authority of which the cargo or freight in question

(*a*) has been arrested to secure such payment, or

(*b*) could have been so arrested, but bail or other security has been given ;

provided that this provision shall apply only if it is claimed that the defendant has an interest in the cargo or freight or had such an interest at the time of salvage ;

(8) in proceedings—

(a) concerning a debt secured on immovable property ;

or

(b) which are brought to assert, declare or determine proprietary or possessory rights, or rights of security, in or over movable property, or to obtain authority to dispose of movable property,

in the courts of the part of the United Kingdom in which the property is situated.

ARTICLE 5A

Proceedings which have as their object a decision of an organ of a company or other legal person or of an association of natural or legal persons may, without prejudice to the other provisions of this Title, be brought in the courts of the part of the United Kingdom in which that company, legal person or association has its seat.

ARTICLE 6

A person domiciled in a **part of the United Kingdom** may, **in another part of the United Kingdom,** also be sued:

(1) where he is one of a number of defendants, in the courts for the place where any one of them is domiciled;

(2) as a third party in an action on a warranty or guarantee or in any other third party proceedings, in the court seised of the original proceedings, unless these were instituted solely with the object of removing him from the jurisdiction of the court which would be competent in his case ;

(3) on a counterclaim arising from the same contract or facts on which the original claim was based, in the court in which the original claim is pending.

ARTICLE 6A

Where by virtue of this **Title** a court of a **part of the United Kingdom** has jurisdiction in actions relating to liability arising from the use or operation of a ship, that court, or any other court substituted for this purpose by the internal law of that **part,** shall also have jurisdiction over claims for limitation of such liability.

. . . .

Section 4

Jurisdiction over consumer contracts

ARTICLE 13

In proceedings concerning a contract concluded by a person for a purpose which can be regarded as being outside his trade or profession, hereinafter called " the consumer ", jurisdiction shall be determined by this Section, without prejudice to the provisions of Articles . . . 5(5) **and (8)(b)**, if it is:

(1) a contract for the sale of goods on instalment credit terms, or

(2) a contract for a loan repayable by instalments, or for any other form of credit, made to finance the sale of goods, or

(3) any other contract for the supply of goods or a contract for the supply of services and . . . the consumer took in **the part of the United Kingdom in which he is domiciled** the steps necessary for the conclusion of the contract.

. . . .

This Section shall not apply to contracts of transport **or insurance.**

ARTICLE 14

A consumer may bring proceedings against the other party to a contract either in the courts of the **part of the United Kingdom** in

SCH. 4 which that party is domiciled or in the courts of the **part of the United Kingdom** in which he is himself domiciled.

Proceedings may be brought against a consumer by the other party to the contract only in the courts of the **part of the United Kingdom** in which the consumer is domiciled.

These provisions shall not affect the right to bring a counterclaim in the court in which, in accordance with this Section, the original claim is pending.

ARTICLE 15

The provisions of this Section may be departed from only by an agreement:

(1) which is entered into after the dispute has arisen,
or

(2) which allows the consumer to bring proceedings in courts other than those indicated in this Section,
or

(3) which is entered into by the consumer and the other party to the contract, both of whom are at the time of conclusion of the contract domiciled or habitually resident in the same **part of the United Kingdom,** and which confers jurisdiction on the courts of that **part,** provided that such an agreement is not contrary to the law of that **part.**

Section 5

Exclusive jurisdiction

ARTICLE 16

The following courts shall have exclusive jurisdiction, regardless of domicile:

(1) in proceedings which have as their object rights *in rem* in, or tenancies of, immovable property, the courts of the **part of the United Kingdom** in which the property is situated;

(2) in proceedings which have as their object the validity of the constitution, the nullity or the dissolution of companies or other legal persons or associations of natural or legal persons . . . the courts of the **part of the United Kingdom** in which the company, legal person or association has its seat;

(3) in proceedings which have as their object the validity of entries in public registers, the courts of the **part of the United Kingdom** in which the register is kept;

. . . .

(5) in proceedings concerned with the enforcement of judgments, the courts of the **part of the United Kingdom** in which the judgment has been or is to be enforced.

Section 6

Prorogation of jurisdiction

ARTICLE 17

If the parties . . . have agreed that a court or the courts of a **part of the United Kingdom** are to have jurisdiction to settle any disputes which have arisen or which may arise in connection with a particular legal relationship, **and, apart from this Schedule, the agreement would be effective to confer jurisdiction under the law of that part,** that court or those courts shall have . . . jurisdiction . . .

The court or courts of a **part of the United Kingdom** on which a trust instrument has conferred jurisdiction shall have . . . jurisdiction in any proceedings brought against a settlor, trustee or beneficiary, if relations between these persons or their rights or obligations under the trust are involved.

Agreements or provisions of a trust instrument conferring jurisdiction shall have no legal force if they are contrary to the provisions of Article . . . 15, or if the courts whose jurisdiction they purport to exclude have exclusive jurisdiction by virtue of Article 16.

. . . .

ARTICLE 18

Apart from jurisdiction derived from other provisions of this **Title,** a court of a **part of the United Kingdom** before whom a defendant enters an appearance shall have jurisdiction. This rule shall not apply where appearance was entered solely to contest the jurisdiction, or where another court has exclusive jurisdiction by virtue of Article 16.

Section 7

Examination as to jurisdiction and admissibility

ARTICLE 19

Where a court of a **part of the United Kingdom** is seised of a claim which is principally concerned with a matter over which the courts of another **part of the United Kingdom** have exclusive jurisdiction by virtue of Article 16, it shall declare of its own motion that it has no jurisdiction.

ARTICLE 20

Where a defendant domiciled in one **part of the United Kingdom** is sued in a court of another **part of the United Kingdom** and does not enter an appearance, the court shall declare of its own motion that it has no jurisdiction unless its jurisdiction is derived from the provisions of this **Title.**

The court shall stay the proceedings so long as it is not shown that the defendant has been able to receive the document instituting the proceedings or an equivalent document in sufficient time to enable him to arrange for his defence, or that all necessary steps have been taken to this end.

. . . .

SCH. 4

Section 9

Provisional, including protective, measures

ARTICLE 24

Application may be made to the courts of a **part of the United Kingdom** for such provisional, including protective, measures as may be available under the law of that **part,** even if, under this **Title,** the courts of another **part of the United Kingdom** have jurisdiction as to the substance of the matter.

Section 17.

SCHEDULE 5

PROCEEDINGS EXCLUDED FROM SCHEDULE 4

Proceedings under the Companies Acts

1948 c. 38. 1960 c. 22 (N.I.).

1. Proceedings for the winding up of a company under the Companies Act 1948 or the Companies Act (Northern Ireland) 1960, or proceedings relating to a company as respects which jurisdiction is conferred on the court having winding up jurisdiction under either of those Acts.

Patents, trade marks, designs and similar rights

2. Proceedings concerned with the registration or validity of patents, trade marks, designs or other similar rights required to be deposited or registered.

Protection of Trading Interests Act 1980

1980 c. 11.

3. Proceedings under section 6 of the Protection of Trading Interests Act 1980 (recovery of sums paid or obtained pursuant to a judgment for multiple damages).

Appeals etc. from tribunals

4. Proceedings on appeal from, or for review of, decisions of tribunals.

Maintenance and similar payments to local and other public authorities

5. Proceedings for, or otherwise relating to, an order under any of the following provisions—

1980 c. 5. 1968 c. 49. 1968 c. 34 (N.I.).

(*a*) section 47 or 51 of the Child Care Act 1980, section 80 of the Social Work (Scotland) Act 1968 or section 156 of the Children and Young Persons Act (Northern Ireland) 1968 (contributions in respect of children in care, etc.);

(*b*) section 49 or 50 of the Child Care Act 1980, section 81 of the Social Work (Scotland) Act 1968 or section 159 of the Children and Young Persons Act (Northern Ireland) 1968 (applications for, or for variation of, affiliation orders in respect of children in care, etc.);

(*c*) section 43 of the National Assistance Act 1948, section 18 of the Supplementary Benefits Act 1976, Article 101 of the Health and Personal Social Services (Northern Ireland) Order 1972 or Article 23 of the Supplementary Benefits (Northern Ireland) Order 1977 (recovery of cost of assistance or benefit from person liable to maintain the assisted person) ; SCH. 5 1948 c. 29. 1976 c. 21. S.I. 1972/1265 (N.I. 14). S.I. 1977/2156 (N.I. 27).

(*d*) section 44 of the National Assistance Act 1948, section 19 of the Supplementary Benefits Act 1976, Article 102 of the Health and Personal Social Services (Northern Ireland) Order 1972 or Article 24 of the Supplementary Benefits (Northern Ireland) Order 1977 (applications for, or for variation of, affiliation orders in respect of children for whom assistance or benefit provided).

Proceedings under certain conventions, etc.

6. Proceedings brought in any court in pursuance of—

(*a*) any statutory provision which, in the case of any convention to which Article 57 applies (conventions relating to specific matters which override the general rules in the 1968 Convention), implements the convention or makes provision with respect to jurisdiction in any field to which the convention relates ; and

(*b*) any rule of law so far as it has the effect of implementing any such convention.

Certain Admiralty proceedings in Scotland

7. Proceedings in Scotland in an Admiralty cause where the jurisdiction of the Court of Session or, as the case may be, of the sheriff is based on arrestment *in rem* or *ad fundandam jurisdictionem* of a ship, cargo or freight.

Register of aircraft mortgages

8. Proceedings for the rectification of the register of aircraft mortgages kept by the Civil Aviation Authority.

Continental Shelf Act 1964

9. Proceedings brought in any court in pursuance of an order under section 3 of the Continental Shelf Act 1964. 1964 c. 29.

SCHEDULE 6

Section 18.

ENFORCEMENT OF U.K. JUDGMENTS (MONEY PROVISIONS)

Preliminary

1. In this Schedule—

"judgment" means any judgment to which section 18 applies and references to the giving of a judgment shall be construed accordingly ;

Sch. 6

" money provision " means a provision for the payment of one or more sums of money ;

" prescribed " means prescribed by rules of court.

Certificates in respect of judgments

2.—(1) Any interested party who wishes to secure the enforcement in another part of the United Kingdom of any money provisions contained in a judgment may apply for a certificate under this Schedule.

(2) The application shall be made in the prescribed manner to the proper officer of the original court, that is to say—

(*a*) in relation to a judgment within paragraph (*a*) of the definition of " judgment " in section 18(2), the court by which the judgment or order was given or made ;

(*b*) in relation to a judgment within paragraph (*b*) of that definition, the court in which the judgment or order is entered ;

(*c*) in relation to a judgment within paragraph (*c*) of that definition, the court in whose books the document is registered ;

(*d*) in relation to a judgment within paragraph (*d*) of that definition, the tribunal by which the award or order was made ;

(*e*) in relation to a judgment within paragraph (*e*) of that definition, the court which gave the judgment or made the order by virtue of which the award has become enforceable as mentioned in that paragraph.

3. A certificate shall not be issued under this Schedule in respect of a judgment unless under the law of the part of the United Kingdom in which the judgment was given—

(*a*) either—

(i) the time for bringing an appeal against the judgment has expired, no such appeal having been brought within that time ; or

(ii) such an appeal having been brought within that time, that appeal has been finally disposed of ; and

(*b*) enforcement of the judgment is not for the time being stayed or suspended, and the time available for its enforcement has not expired.

4.—(1) Subject to paragraph 3, on an application under paragraph 2 the proper officer shall issue to the applicant a certificate in the prescribed form—

(*a*) stating the sum or aggregate of the sums (including any costs or expenses) payable under the money provisions contained in the judgment, the rate of interest, if any, payable thereon and the date or time from which any such interest began to accrue ;

(*b*) stating that the conditions specified in paragraph 3(*a*) and (*b*) are satisfied in relation to the judgment ; and

(*c*) containing such other particulars as may be prescribed.

(2) More than one certificate may be issued under this Schedule (simultaneously or at different times) in respect of the same judgment. SCH. 6

Registration of certificates

5.—(1) Where a certificate has been issued under this Schedule in any part of the United Kingdom, any interested party may, within six months from the date of its issue, apply in the prescribed manner to the proper officer of the superior court in any other part of the United Kingdom for the certificate to be registered in that court.

(2) In this paragraph "superior court" means, in relation to England and Wales or Northern Ireland, the High Court and, in relation to Scotland, the Court of Session.

(3) Where an application is duly made under this paragraph to the proper officer of a superior court, he shall register the certificate in that court in the prescribed manner.

General effect of registration

6.—(1) A certificate registered under this Schedule shall, for the purposes of its enforcement, be of the same force and effect, the registering court shall have in relation to its enforcement the same powers, and proceedings for or with respect to its enforcement may be taken, as if the certificate had been a judgment originally given in the registering court and had (where relevant) been entered.

(2) Sub-paragraph (1) is subject to the following provisions of this Schedule and to any provision made by rules of court as to the manner in which and the conditions subject to which a certificate registered under this Schedule may be enforced.

Costs or expenses

7. Where a certificate is registered under this Schedule, the reasonable costs or expenses of and incidental to the obtaining of the certificate and its registration shall be recoverable as if they were costs or expenses stated in the certificate to be payable under a money provision contained in the original judgment.

Interest

8.—(1) Subject to any provision made under sub-paragraph (2), the debt resulting, apart from paragraph 7, from the registration of the certificate shall carry interest at the rate, if any, stated in the certificate from the date or time so stated.

(2) Provision may be made by rules of court as to the manner in which and the periods by reference to which any interest payable by virtue of sub-paragraph (1) is to be calculated and paid, including provision for such interest to cease to accrue as from a prescribed date.

(3) All such sums as are recoverable by virtue of paragraph 7 carry interest as if they were the subject of an order for costs or expenses made by the registering court on the date of registration of the certificate.

SCH. 6

(4) Except as provided by this paragraph sums payable by virtue of the registration of a certificate under this Schedule shall not carry interest.

Stay or sisting of enforcement in certain cases

9. Where a certificate in respect of a judgment has been registered under this Schedule, the registering court may, if it is satisfied that any person against whom it is sought to enforce the certificate is entitled and intends to apply under the law of the part of the United Kingdom in which the judgment was given for any remedy which would result in the setting aside or quashing of the judgment, stay (or, in Scotland, sist) proceedings for the enforcement of the certificate, on such terms as it thinks fit, for such period as appears to the court to be reasonably sufficient to enable the application to be disposed of.

Cases in which registration of a certificate must or may be set aside

10. Where a certificate has been registered under this Schedule, the registering court—

(*a*) shall set aside the registration if, on an application made by any interested party, it is satisfied that the registration was contrary to the provisions of this Schedule ;

(*b*) may set aside the registration if, on an application so made, it is satisfied that the matter in dispute in the proceedings in which the judgment in question was given had previously been the subject of a judgment by another court or tribunal having jurisdiction in the matter.

Section 18.

SCHEDULE 7

ENFORCEMENT OF U.K. JUDGMENTS (NON-MONEY PROVISIONS)

Preliminary

1. In this Schedule—

" judgment " means any judgment to which section 18 applies and references to the giving of a judgment shall be construed accordingly ;

" non-money provision " means a provision for any relief or remedy not requiring payment of a sum of money ;

" prescribed " means prescribed by rules of court.

Certified copies of judgments

2.—(1) Any interested party who wishes to secure the enforcement in another part of the United Kingdom of any non-money provisions contained in a judgment may apply for a certified copy of the judgment.

(2) The application shall be made in the prescribed manner to the proper officer of the original court, that is to say—

(*a*) in relation to a judgment within paragraph (*a*) of the definition of " judgment " in section 18(2), the court by which the judgment or order was given or made ;

(*b*) in relation to a judgment within paragraph (*b*) of that definition, the court in which the judgment or order is entered ; SCH. 7

(*c*) in relation to a judgment within paragraph (*c*) of that definition, the court in whose books the document is registered ;

(*d*) in relation to a judgment within paragraph (*d*) of that definition, the tribunal by which the award or order was made ;

(*e*) in relation to a judgment within paragraph (*e*) of that definition, the court which gave the judgment or made the order by virtue of which the award has become enforceable as mentioned in that paragraph.

3. A certified copy of a judgment shall not be issued under this Schedule unless under the law of the part of the United Kingdom in which the judgment was given—

(*a*) either—

(i) the time for bringing an appeal against the judgment has expired, no such appeal having been brought within that time ; or

(ii) such an appeal having been brought within that time, that appeal has been finally disposed of ; and

(*b*) enforcement of the judgment is not for the time being stayed or suspended, and the time available for its enforcement has not expired.

4.—(1) Subject to paragraph 3, on an application under paragraph 2 the proper officer shall issue to the applicant—

(*a*) a certified copy of the judgment (including any money provisions or excepted provisions which it may contain) ; and

(*b*) a certificate stating that the conditions specified in paragraph 3(*a*) and (*b*) are satisfied in relation to the judgment.

(2) In sub-paragraph (1)(*a*) " excepted provision " means any provision of a judgment which is excepted from the application of section 18 by subsection (5) of that section.

(3) There may be issued under this Schedule (simultaneously or at different times)—

(*a*) more than one certified copy of the same judgment ; and

(*b*) more than one certificate in respect of the same judgment.

Registration of judgments

5.—(1) Where a certified copy of a judgment has been issued under this Schedule in any part of the United Kingdom, any interested party may apply in the prescribed manner to the superior court in any other part of the United Kingdom for the judgment to be registered in that court.

(2) In this paragraph " superior court " means, in relation to England and Wales or Northern Ireland, the High Court and, in relation to Scotland, the Court of Session.

SCH. 7

(3) An application under this paragraph for the registration of a judgment must be accompanied by—

(*a*) a certified copy of the judgment issued under this Schedule ; and

(*b*) a certificate issued under paragraph 4(1)(*b*) in respect of the judgment not more than six months before the date of the application.

(4) Subject to sub-paragraph (5), where an application under this paragraph is duly made to a superior court, the court shall order the whole of the judgment as set out in the certified copy to be registered in that court in the prescribed manner.

(5) A judgment shall not be registered under this Schedule by the superior court in any part of the United Kingdom if compliance with the non-money provisions contained in the judgment would involve a breach of the law of that part of the United Kingdom.

General effect of registration

6.—(1) The non-money provisions contained in a judgment registered under this Schedule shall, for the purposes of their enforcement, be of the same force and effect, the registering court shall have in relation to their enforcement the same powers, and proceedings for or with respect to their enforcement may be taken, as if the judgment containing them had been originally given in the registering court and had (where relevant) been entered.

(2) Sub-paragraph (1) is subject to the following provisions of this Schedule and to any provision made by rules of court as to the manner in which and conditions subject to which the non-money provisions contained in a judgment registered under this Schedule may be enforced.

Costs or expenses

7.—(1) Where a judgment is registered under this Schedule, the reasonable costs or expenses of and incidental to—

(*a*) the obtaining of the certified copy of the judgment and of the necessary certificate under paragraph 4(1)(*b*) in respect of it ; and

(*b*) the registration of the judgment,

shall be recoverable as if on the date of registration there had also been registered in the registering court a certificate under Schedule 6 in respect of the judgment and as if those costs or expenses were costs or expenses stated in that certificate to be payable under a money provision contained in the judgment.

(2) All such sums as are recoverable by virtue of sub-paragraph (1) shall carry interest as if they were the subject of an order for costs or expenses made by the registering court on the date of registration of the judgment.

Stay or sisting of enforcement in certain cases SCH. 7

8. Where a judgment has been registered under this Schedule, the registering court may, if it is satisfied that any person against whom it is sought to enforce the judgment is entitled and intends to apply under the law of the part of the United Kingdom in which the judgment was given for any remedy which would result in the setting aside or quashing of the judgment, stay (or, in Scotland, sist) proceedings for the enforcement of the judgment, on such terms as it thinks fit, for such period as appears to the court to be reasonably sufficient to enable the application to be disposed of.

Cases in which registered judgment must or may be set aside

9. Where a judgment has been registered under this Schedule, the registering court—

(*a*) shall set aside the registration if, on an application made by any interested party, it is satisfied that the registration was contrary to the provisions of this Schedule ;

(*b*) may set aside the registration if, on an application so made, it is satisfied that the matter in dispute in the proceedings in which the judgment was given had previously been the subject of a judgment by another court or tribunal having jurisdiction in the matter.

SCHEDULE 8

Section 20.

RULES AS TO JURISDICTION IN SCOTLAND

General

1. Subject to the **following Rules,** persons shall be sued in the courts **for the place where they are domiciled.** [Article 2]

Special jurisdiction

2. **Subject to Rules 3 (jurisdiction over consumer contracts), 4 (exclusive jurisdiction) and 5 (prorogation)** a person may **also** be sued— [Article 5]

(1) **where he has no fixed residence, in a court within whose jurisdiction he is personally cited ;**

(2) in matters relating to a contract, in the courts for the place of performance of the obligation in question ; [Article 5(1)]

(3) in matters relating to delict or quasi-delict, in the courts for the place where the harmful event occurred ; [Article 5(3)]

(4) as regards a civil claim for damages or restitution which is based on an act giving rise to criminal proceedings, in the court seised of those proceedings to the extent that that court has jurisdiction to entertain civil proceedings ; [Article 5(4)]

(5) in matters relating to maintenance, in the courts for the place where the maintenance creditor is domiciled or habitually resident or, if the matter is ancillary to proceedings concerning the status of a person, in the court which has [Article 5(2)]

SCH. 8

jurisdiction to entertain those proceedings, **provided that an action for adherence and aliment or of affiliation and aliment shall be treated as a matter relating to maintenance which is not ancillary to proceedings concerning the status of a person, and provided also that—**

(a) where a local authority exercises its power to raise an action under section 44(7)(a) of the National Assistance Act 1948 or under section 81(1) of the Social Work (Scotland) Act 1968 ; and 1948 c. 29. 1968 c. 49.

(b) where the Secretary of State exercises his power to raise an action under section 19(8)(a) of the Supplementary Benefits Act 1976 ; 1976 c. 71.

this Rule shall apply as if the reference to the maintenance creditor were a reference to the mother of the child ;

[Article 5(5)] (6) as regards a dispute arising out of the operations of a branch, agency or other establishment, in the courts for the place in which the branch, agency or other establishment is situated ;

[Article 5(6)] (7) in his capacity as settlor, trustee or beneficiary of a trust **domiciled in Scotland** created by the operation of a statute, or by a written instrument, or created orally and evidenced in writing, in the **Court of Session, or the appropriate sheriff court within the meaning of section 24A of the Trusts (Scotland) Act 1921 ;** 1921 c. 58.

(8) **where he is not domiciled in the United Kingdom, in the courts for any place where—**

(a) any moveable property belonging to him has been arrested ; or

(b) any immoveable property in which he has any beneficial interest is situated ;

(9) **in proceedings which are brought to assert, declare or determine proprietary or possessory rights, or rights of security, in or over moveable property, or to obtain authority to dispose of moveable property, in the courts for the place where the property is situated ;**

(10) **in proceedings for interdict, in the courts for the place where it is alleged that the wrong is likely to be committed ;**

(11) **in proceedings concerning a debt secured over immoveable property, in the courts for the place where the property is situated ;**

(12) **in proceedings which have as their object a decision of an organ of a company or other legal person or of an association of natural or legal persons, in the courts for the place where that company, legal person or association has its seat ;**

(13) **in proceedings concerning an arbitration which is conducted in Scotland or in which the procedure is governed by Scots law, in the Court of Session ;**

(14) **in proceedings principally concerned with the registration in the United Kingdom or the validity in the United Kingdom of patents, trade marks, designs or other similar rights required to be deposited or registered, in the Court of Session ;** SCH. 8

(15) (*a*) where he is one of a number of **defenders,** in the courts for the place where any one of them is domiciled ; [Article 6]

(*b*) as a third party in an action on a warranty or guarantee or in any other third party proceedings, in the court seised of the original proceedings, unless these were instituted solely with the object of removing him from the jurisdiction of the court which would be competent in his case ;

(*c*) on a counterclaim arising from the same contract or facts on which the original claim was based, in the court in which the original claim is pending.

Jurisdiction over consumer contracts

3.—(1) In proceedings concerning a contract concluded by a person for a purpose which can be regarded as being outside his trade or profession, hereinafter called the "consumer", **subject to Rule 4 (exclusive jurisdiction),** jurisdiction shall be determined by this **Rule** if it is— [Article 13]

(*a*) a contract for the sale of goods on instalment credit terms ; **or**

(*b*) a contract for a loan repayable by instalments, or for any other form of credit, made to finance the sale of goods ; or

(*c*) any other contract for the supply of goods or a contract for the supply of services, **if**—

(i) the consumer took in **Scotland** the steps necessary for the conclusion of the contract ; **or**

(ii) **proceedings are brought in Scotland by virtue of section 10(3).**

(2) This **Rule** shall not apply to contracts of transport **or contracts of insurance.**

(3) A consumer may bring proceedings against the other party to a contract **only** in— [Article 14]

(*a*) the courts **for the place** in which that party is domiciled ;

(*b*) the courts **for the place** in which he is himself domiciled ; **or**

(*c*) **any court having jurisdiction by virtue of Rule 2(6) or (9).**

(4) Proceedings may be brought against a consumer by the other party to the contract only in the courts **for the place where** the consumer is domiciled **or any court having jurisdiction under Rule 2(9).**

(5) **Nothing in this Rule** shall affect the right to bring a counterclaim in the court in which, **in accordance with this Rule,** the original claim is pending.

SCH. 8

[Article 15(1) and (2)] (6) The provisions of this **Rule** may be departed from only by an agreement—

(*a*) which is entered into after the dispute has arisen ; or

(*b*) which allows the consumer to bring proceedings in **a court** other than **a court** indicated in this **Rule.**

Exclusive jurisdiction

[Article 16] 4.—(1) **Notwithstanding anything contained in any of Rules 1 to 3 above or 5 to 8 below,** the following courts shall have exclusive jurisdiction—

[Article 16(1)] (*a*) in proceedings which have as their object rights *in rem* in, or tenancies of, immoveable property, the courts **for the place where** the property is situated ;

[Article 16(2)] (*b*) in proceedings which have as their object the validity of the constitution, the nullity or the dissolution of companies or other legal persons or associations of natural or legal persons, the courts **for the place where** the company, legal person or association has its seat ;

[Article 16(3)] (*c*) in proceedings which have as their object the validity of entries in public registers, the courts **for the place where** the register is kept ;

[Article 16(5)] (*d*) in proceedings concerned with the enforcement of judgements, the courts **for the place where** the judgement has been or is to be enforced.

(2) **Nothing in paragraph (1)(c) above affects jurisdiction in any proceedings concerning the validity of entries in registers of patents, trade marks, designs, or other similar rights required to be deposited or registered.**

(3) **No court shall exercise jurisdiction in a case where immoveable property, the seat of a body mentioned in paragraph (1)(b) above, a public register or the place where a judgement has been or is to be enforced is situated outside Scotland and where paragraph (1) above would apply if the property, seat, register or, as the case may be, place of enforcement were situated in Scotland.**

Prorogation of jurisdiction

[Article 17(1)] 5.—(1) If the parties have agreed that a court is to have jurisdiction to settle any disputes which have arisen or which may arise in connection with a particular legal relationship, that court shall have exclusive jurisdiction.

[Article 17(1)] (2) Such an agreement conferring jurisdiction shall be either in writing or evidenced in writing or, in trade or commerce, in a form which accords with practices in that trade or commerce of which the parties are or ought to have been aware.

[Article 17(2)] (3) The court on which a trust instrument has conferred jurisdiction shall have exclusive jurisdiction in any proceedings brought against a settlor, trustee or beneficiary, if relations between these persons or their rights or obligations under the trust are involved.

(4) **Where an agreement or a trust instrument confers jurisdiction on the courts of the United Kingdom or of Scotland, proceedings to which paragraph (1) or, as the case may be, (3) above applies may be brought in any court in Scotland.** SCH. 8

(5) Agreements or provisions of a trust instrument conferring jurisdiction shall have no legal force if the courts whose jurisdiction they purport to exclude have exclusive jurisdiction by virtue of **Rule 4 or where Rule 4(3) applies.** [Article 17(3)]

6.—(1) Apart from jurisdiction derived from other provisions of this **Schedule,** a court before whom a defender enters an appearance shall have jurisdiction. [Article 18]

(2) This Rule shall not apply where appearance was entered solely to contest jurisdiction, or where another court has exclusive jurisdiction by virtue of **Rule 4 or where Rule 4(3) applies.**

Examination as to jurisdiction and admissibility

7. Where a court is seised of a claim which is principally concerned with a matter over which **another court has** exclusive jurisdiction by virtue of **Rule 4, or where it is precluded from exercising jurisdiction by Rule 4(3),** it shall declare of its own motion that it has no jurisdiction. [Article 19]

8. Where **in any case a court has no jurisdiction which is compatible with this Act, and the defender** does not enter an appearance, the court shall declare of its own motion that it has no jurisdiction. [Article 20]

SCHEDULE 9

Section 21.

PROCEEDINGS EXCLUDED FROM SCHEDULE 8

1. Proceedings concerning the status or legal capacity of natural persons (including proceedings for separation) other than proceedings which consist solely of proceedings for adherence and aliment or of affiliation and aliment.

2. Proceedings for regulating the custody of children.

3. Proceedings relating to tutory and curatory and all proceedings relating to the management of the affairs of persons who are incapable of managing their own affairs.

4. Proceedings in respect of sequestration in bankruptcy ; or the winding up of a company or other legal person ; or proceedings in respect of a judicial arrangement or judicial composition with creditors.

5. Proceedings relating to a company where, by any enactment, jurisdiction in respect of those proceedings is conferred on the court having jurisdiction to wind it up.

6. Admiralty causes in so far as the jurisdiction is based on arrestment *in rem* or *ad fundandam jurisdictionem* of a ship, cargo or freight.

SCH. 9

7. Commissary proceedings.

8. Proceedings for the rectification of the register of aircraft mortgages kept by the Civil Aviation Authority.

1962 c. 8. 9. Proceedings under section 7(3) of the Civil Aviation (Eurocontrol) Act 1962 (recovery of charges for air navigation services and proceedings for damages against Eurocontrol).

10. Proceedings brought in pursuance of an order under section
1964 c. 29. 3 of the Continental Shelf Act 1964.

1980 c. 11. 11. Proceedings under section 6 of the Protection of Trading Interests Act 1980 (recovery of sums paid or obtained pursuant to a judgment for multiple damages).

12. Appeals from or review of decisions of tribunals.

13. Proceedings which are not in substance proceedings in which a decree against any person is sought.

14. Proceedings brought in any court in pursuance of—

(*a*) any statutory provision which, in the case of any convention to which Article 57 applies (conventions relating to specific matters which override the general rules in the 1968 Convention), implements the convention ; and

(*b*) any rule of law so far as it has the effect of implementing any such convention.

Section 35(1)

SCHEDULE 10

1933 c. 13.

AMENDMENTS OF FOREIGN JUDGMENTS (RECIPROCAL ENFORCEMENT) ACT 1933

1.—(1) Section 1 (power to extend Part I to foreign countries giving reciprocal treatment) is amended as follows.

(2) For subsections (1) and (2) substitute—

"(1) If, in the case of any foreign country, Her Majesty is satisfied that, in the event of the benefits conferred by this Part of this Act being extended to, or to any particular class of, judgments given in the courts of that country or in any particular class of those courts, substantial reciprocity of treatment will be assured as regards the enforcement in that country of similar judgments given in similar courts of the United Kingdom, She may by Order in Council direct—

(*a*) that this Part of this Act shall extend to that country ;

(*b*) that such courts of that country as are specified in the Order shall be recognised courts of that country for the purposes of this Part of this Act ; and

(*c*) that judgments of any such recognised court, or such judgments of any class so specified, shall, if within subsection (2) of this section, be judgments to which this Part of this Act applies.

(2) Subject to subsection (2A) of this section, a judgment of a recognised court is within this subsection if it satisfies the following conditions, namely— Sch. 10

(*a*) it is either final and conclusive as between the judgment debtor and the judgment creditor or requires the former to make an interim payment to the latter ; and

(*b*) there is payable under it a sum of money, not being a sum payable in respect of taxes or other charges of a like nature or in respect of a fine or other penalty ; and

(*c*) it is given after the coming into force of the Order in Council which made that court a recognised court.

(2A) The following judgments of a recognised court are not within subsection (2) of this section—

(*a*) a judgment given by that court on appeal from a court which is not a recognised court ;

(*b*) a judgment or other instrument which is regarded for the purposes of its enforcement as a judgment of that court but which was given or made in another country ;

(*c*) a judgment given by that court in proceedings founded on a judgment of a court in another country and having as their object the enforcement of that judgment.".

(3) After subsection (4) add—

"(5) Any Order in Council made under this section before its amendment by the Civil Jurisdiction and Judgments Act 1982 which deems any court of a foreign country to be a superior court of that country for the purposes of this Part of this Act shall (without prejudice to subsection (4) of this section) have effect from the time of that amendment as if it provided for that court to be a recognised court of that country for those purposes, and for any final and conclusive judgment of that court, if within subsection (2) of this section, to be a judgment to which this Part of this Act applies.".

2. In section 9 (power to make foreign judgments unenforceable in United Kingdom if no reciprocity), in subsection (1) omit "superior" in both places where it occurs.

3. For section 10 (issue of certificates of judgments obtained in the United Kingdom) substitute—

"Provision for issue of copies of, and certificates in connection with, U.K. judgments.

10.—(1) Rules may make provision for enabling any judgment creditor wishing to secure the enforcement in a foreign country to which Part I of this Act extends of a judgment to which this subsection applies, to obtain, subject to any conditions specified in the rules—

(*a*) a copy of the judgment ; and

(*b*) a certificate giving particulars relating to the judgment and the proceedings in which it was given.

(2) Subsection (1) applies to any judgment given by a court or tribunal in the United Kingdom under which a

SCH. 10

sum of money is payable, not being a sum payable in respect of taxes or other charges of a like nature or in respect of a fine or other penalty.

(3) In this section " rules "—

(*a*) in relation to judgments given by a court, means rules of court;

(*b*) in relation to judgments given by any other tribunal, means rules or regulations made by the authority having power to make rules or regulations regulating the procedure of that tribunal.".

4. After section 10 insert—

"Arbitration awards. 10A. The provisions of this Act, except sections 1(5) and 6, shall apply, as they apply to a judgment, in relation to an award in proceedings on an arbitration which has, in pursuance of the law in force in the place where it was made, become enforceable in the same manner as a judgment given by a court in that place.".

5.—(1) Section 11(1) (interpretation) is amended as follows.

(2) After the definition of " Country of the original court " insert—

" " Court ", except in section 10 of this Act, includes a tribunal; ".

(3) Omit the definition of " Judgments given in the superior courts of the United Kingdom ".

Section 37(1).

SCHEDULE 11

MINOR AMENDMENTS RELATING TO MAINTENANCE ORDERS

PART I

ENFORCEMENT OF LUMP SUM ORDERS

Maintenance Orders Act 1950 (*c.* 37)

1. In section 18(3A) of the Maintenance Orders Act 1950 (order not to be enforced by registering court under that Act if re-registered for enforcement in another court), for " whilst it is registered " substitute " to the extent that it is for the time being registered ".

Maintenance Orders Act 1958 (*c.* 39)

2.—(1) Section 2 of the Maintenance Orders Act 1958 (registration of orders) is amended as follows.

(2) In subsection (3) (registration of magistrates' court order for enforcement in the High Court), for the words from " shall " onwards (which require the court to be satisfied that not less than a certain number of periodical payments are in arrears) substitute " may, if it thinks fit, grant the application ".

(3) After subsection (3) insert—

" (3A) Without prejudice to subsection (3) of this section, where a magistrates' court order provides both for the payment of a lump sum and for the making of periodical payments, a person entitled to receive a lump sum under the order who considers that, so far as it relates to that sum, the order could be more effectively enforced if it were registered may apply to the original court for the registration of the order so far as it so relates, and the court may, if it thinks fit, grant the application.

(3B) Where an application under subsection (3A) of this section is granted in the case of a magistrates' court order, the provisions of this Part of this Act shall have effect in relation to that order as if so far as it relates to the payment of a lump sum it were a separate order.".

Maintenance and Affiliation Orders Act (Northern Ireland) 1966 (*c.* 35) (*N.I.*)

3.—(1) Section 11 of the Maintenance and Affiliation Orders Act (Northern Ireland) 1966 (registration of orders) is amended as follows.

(2) In subsection (3) (registration of order made by court of summary jurisdiction for enforcement in the High Court), for the words from " shall " onwards (which require the court to be satisfied that not less than a certain number of periodical payments are in arrears) substitute " may, if it thinks fit, grant the application ".

(3) After subsection (3) insert—

" (3A) Without prejudice to subsection (3), where an order made by a court of summary jurisdiction provides both for the payment of a lump sum and for the making of periodical payments, a person entitled to receive a lump sum under the order who considers that, so far as it relates to that sum the order could be more effectively enforced if it were registered may apply to the original court for the registration of the order so far as it so relates, and the court may, if it thinks fit, grant the application.

(3B) Where an application under subsection (3A) is granted in the case of an order made by a court of summary jurisdiction, the provisions of this Part shall have effect in relation to that order as if so far as it relates to the payment of a lump sum it were a separate order.".

Maintenance Orders (Reciprocal Enforcement) Act 1972 *(c.* 18*)*

4.—(1) In section 9 of the Maintenance Orders (Reciprocal Enforcement) Act 1972 (variation and revocation of orders), after subsection (1) insert—

" (1A) The powers conferred by subsection (1) above are not exercisable in relation to so much of a registered order as provides for the payment of a lump sum.".

SCH. 11

(2) In section 21 of that Act (interpretation of Part I)—

(*a*) in paragraph (*a*) of the definition of " maintenance order " in subsection (1) ; and

(*b*) in subsection (2),

for " periodical payment of sums of money " substitute " payment of a lump sum or the making of periodical payments ".

PART II

RECOVERY OF INTEREST ON ARREARS

Maintenance Orders Act 1950 *(c.* 37*)*

5. In section 18 of the Maintenance Orders Act 1950 (enforcement of registered orders), after subsection (1) (orders to be enforced in the same manner as orders made by the court of registration), insert—

" (1A) A maintenance order registered under this Part of this Act in a court of summary jurisdiction in England or Northern Ireland shall not carry interest ; but where a maintenance order so registered is registered in the High Court under Part I of the Maintenance Orders Act 1958 or section 36 of the Civil Jurisdiction and Judgments Act 1982, this subsection shall not prevent any sum for whose payment the order provides from carrying interest in accordance with section 2A of the said Act of 1958 or section 11A of the Maintenance and Affiliation Orders Act (Northern Ireland) 1966.

(1B) A maintenance order made in Scotland which is registered under this Part of this Act in the Supreme Court in England or Northern Ireland shall, if interest is by the law of Scotland recoverable under the order, carry the like interest in accordance with subsection (1) of this section.".

Maintenance Orders Act 1958 *(c.* 39*)*

6. (1) The Maintenance Orders Act 1958 is amended as follows.

(2) After section 2 insert—

"Interest on sums recoverable under certain orders registered in the High Court.

2A.—(1) Where, in connection with an application under section 2(3) of this Act for the registration of a magistrates' court order, the applicant shows in accordance with rules of court—

(*a*) that the order, though deemed for the purposes of section 1 of this Act to have been made by a magistrates' court in England, was in fact made in another part of the United Kingdom or in a country or territory outside the United Kingdom ; and

(*b*) that, as regards any sum for whose payment the order provides, interest on that sum at a particular rate is, by the law of that part or of that country or territory, recoverable under the order from a particular date or time, then, if the original court grants the application and causes a certified copy of the order to be sent to the prescribed officer of the High Court under section 2(4)(*c*) of this Act, it shall also cause to be sent to him a certificate in the prescribed form showing, as regards that sum, the rate of interest so recoverable and the date or time from which it is so recoverable.

(2) The officer of the court who receives a certificate sent to him under the preceding subsection shall cause the certificate to be registered in that court together with the order to which it relates.

(3) Where an order is registered together with a certificate under this section, then, subject to any provision made under the next following subsection, sums payable under the order shall carry interest at the rate specified in the certificate from the date or time so specified.

(4) Provision may be made by rules of court as to the manner in which and the periods by reference to which any interest payable by virtue of subsection (3) is to be calculated and paid, including provision for such interest to cease to accrue as from a prescribed date.

(5) Except as provided by this section sums payable under registered orders shall not carry interest.".

(3) In section 3(1) of that Act (enforcement of registered orders), after " Subject to the provisions of " insert " section 2A of this Act and ".

Maintenance and Affiliation Orders Act (Northern Ireland) 1966 *(c. 35) (N.I.)*

7.—(1) The Maintenance and Affiliation Orders Act (Northern Ireland) 1966 is amended as follows.

(2) After section 11 insert—

"Interest on sums recoverable under certain orders registered in the High Court.

11A.—(1) Where, in connection with an application under section 11(3) for the registration of an order made by a court of summary jurisdiction, the applicant shows in accordance with rules of court—

(*a*) that the order, though deemed for the purposes of this Part to have been made by a court of summary jurisdiction in Northern Ireland, was in fact made in a country or territory outside the United Kingdom ; and

(*b*) that, as regards any sum for whose payment the order provides, interest on that sum at a particular rate is, by the law of that country or territory, recoverable under the order from a particular date or time,

then, if the original court grants the application and causes a certified copy of the order to be sent to the

SCH. 11

prescribed officer of the High Court under section 11(4)(*c*) it shall also cause to be sent to him a certificate in the prescribed form showing, as regards that sum, the rate of interest so recoverable and the date or time from which it is so recoverable.

(2) The officer of a court who receives a certificate sent to him under subsection (1) shall cause the certificate to be registered in that court together with the order to which it relates.

(3) Where an order is registered together with a certificate under this section, then, subject to any provision made under subsection (4), sums payable under the order shall carry interest at the rate specified in the certificate from the date or time so specified.

(4) Provision may be made by rules of court as to the manner in which and the periods by reference to which any interest payable by virtue of subsection (3) is to be calculated and paid, including provision for such interest to cease to accrue as from a prescribed date.

(5) Except as provided by this section sums payable under registered orders shall not carry interest.".

(3) In section 12(1) (enforcement of registered orders), after " Subject to the provisions of " insert " section 11A and ".

(4) In section 16(2) of that Act (construction of " rules of court ") at the end add " and in section 11A(4) shall be construed as including a reference to Judgment Enforcement Rules made under Article 141 of the Judgments Enforcement (Northern Ireland) Order 1981 ".

PART III

RECIPROCAL ENFORCEMENT FOUNDED ON PRESENCE OF ASSETS

Maintenance Orders (Reciprocal Enforcement) Act 1972 *(c.* 18*)*

8. The Maintenance Orders (Reciprocal Enforcement) Act 1972 is amended as follows.

9. In section 2 (transmission of United Kingdom order for enforcement in reciprocating country)—

(*a*) in subsections (1) and (4), after " residing " insert " or has assets " ; and

(*b*) in subsection (4), after " whereabouts of the payer ", in both places where it occurs, insert " and the nature and location of his assets in that country ".

10. In section 6 (registration in United Kingdom of order made in reciprocating country)—

(*a*) in subsection (2), after " residing " insert " or has assets " ; and (*b*) in subsection (4)— SCH. 11

(i) after " is residing " insert " or has assets " ;

(ii) for " so residing " substitute " residing and has no assets within the jurisdiction of the court " ; and

(iii) at the end insert " and the nature and location of his assets ".

11. In section 8(5) (duty of magistrates' court and its officers to take prescribed steps for enforcing registered orders), after " enforcing " insert " or facilitating the enforcement of ".

12. In section 9 (variation and revocation of orders), after the subsection (1A) inserted by paragraph 4(1) of this Schedule, insert—

"(1B) The registering court shall not vary or revoke a registered order if neither the payer nor the payee under the order is resident in the United Kingdom.".

13.—(1) Section 10 (cancellation of registration and transfer of orders) is amended as follows.

(2) In subsection (2), for " has ceased to reside within the jurisdiction of that court," substitute " is not residing within the jurisdiction of that court and has no assets within that jurisdiction against which the order can be effectively enforced,".

(3) In subsection (3), after " residing " insert " or has assets ".

(4) In subsection (5), for " still residing " substitute " residing or has assets ".

(5) In subsection (6)—

(*a*) after " is residing " insert " or has assets " ; and

(*b*) for " so residing " insert " residing and has no assets within the jurisdiction of the court ".

(6) In subsection (7)(*b*), after " payer " insert " and the nature and location of his assets ".

14. In section 11(1) (steps to be taken where payer is not residing in the United Kingdom)—

(*a*) before " it appears " insert " at any time " ;

(*b*) for the words from " in the United Kingdom " to " therein, " substitute " and has no assets in the United Kingdom," ; and

(*c*) after " payer " in paragraph (*c*) insert " and the nature and location of his assets ".

15. In section 21(1) (interpretation of Part I), in the definition of " the appropriate court "—

(i) after " residing ", in the first and second places where it occurs, insert " or having assets " ;

SCH. 11

(ii) for " the sheriff court " substitute " a sheriff court " ; and

(iii) after " residing ", where it last occurs, insert " or has assets ".

1920 c. 33.

16. In section 24 (application of Part I to certain orders and proceedings under Maintenance Orders (Facilities for Enforcement) Act 1920), in paragraph (*a*)(i) and (ii), after " residing " insert " or having assets ".

17. In section 40 (power to apply Act with modifications by Order in Council)—

(*a*) in paragraph (*a*), omit " against persons in that country or territory " ; and

(*b*) in paragraph (*b*), omit " against persons in the United Kingdom ".

18. In section 47 (interpretation), in subsection (3) (construction of references to a court's jurisdiction), after " the reference is " insert " to assets being located or " and omit the words " or having ceased to reside ".

Sections 15(4), 23(2) and 36(6).

SCHEDULE 12

CONSEQUENTIAL AMENDMENTS

PART I

AMENDMENTS CONSEQUENTIAL ON PART I OF THIS ACT

Army Act 1955 (*c.* 18) *and Air Force Act* 1955 (*c.* 19)

1. In section 150 of the Army Act 1955 and in section 150 of the Air Force Act 1955 (enforcement of maintenance and other orders by deduction from pay), in subsection (5), after " Part I of the Maintenance Orders (Reciprocal Enforcement) Act 1972 " insert " or Part I of the Civil Jurisdiction and Judgments Act 1982 ".

Naval Discipline Act 1957 (*c.* 53)

2. In section 101 of the Naval Discipline Act 1957 (service of process in maintenance and other proceedings), in subsection (5), after " Part I of the Maintenance Orders (Reciprocal Enforcement) Act 1972 " insert " or Part I of the Civil Jurisdiction and Judgments Act 1982 ".

Maintenance Orders Act 1958 (*c.* 39)

3. In section 1 of the Maintenance Orders Act 1958 (scope of application of Part I), in subsection (4), for the words from " within the meaning " to " the said Part I " substitute " which is registered in a magistrates' court under Part I of the Maintenance Orders (Reciprocal Enforcement) Act 1972 or Part I of the Civil Jurisdiction and Judgments Act 1982 ".

Maintenance and Affiliation Orders Act (Northern Ireland) 1966 (*c.* 35) (*N.I.*) SCH. 12

4. In section 10 of the Maintenance and Affiliation Orders Act (Northern Ireland) 1966 (orders to which Part II of that Act applies), in subsections (2) and (5), after " Part I of the Maintenance Orders (Reciprocal Enforcement) Act 1972 " insert " or Part I of the Civil Jurisdiction and Judgments Act 1982 ".

Administration of Justice Act 1970 (*c.* 31)

5. In Schedule 8 to the Administration of Justice Act 1970 (orders which are " maintenance orders " for the purposes of Part II of that Act and Part II of the Maintenance Orders Act 1958), after paragraph 12 insert— 1958 c. 39.

" 13. A maintenance order within the meaning of Part I of the Civil Jurisdiction and Judgments Act 1982 which is registered in a magistrates' court under that Part.".

Attachment of Earnings Act 1971 (*c.* 32)

6. In Schedule 1 to the Attachment of Earnings Act 1971 (orders which are " maintenance orders " for the purposes of that Act), after paragraph 12 insert—

" 13. A maintenance order within the meaning of Part I of the Civil Jurisdiction and Judgments Act 1982 which is registered in a magistrates' court under that Part.".

Magistrates' Courts Act 1980 (*c.* 43)

7. In section 65 of the Magistrates' Courts Act 1980 (definition of " domestic proceedings " for the purposes of that Act)—

(*a*) in subsection (1), after paragraph (*l*) insert—

" (*m*) Part I of the Civil Jurisdiction and Judgments Act 1982, so far as that Part relates to the recognition or enforcement of maintenance orders ; " ;

(*b*) in subsection (2)(*a*), after " (*k*) " insert " and (*m*) ".

Magistrates' Courts (Northern Ireland) Order 1981 (*S.I.* 1981/1675 (*N.I.* 26))

8.—(1) In Article 88 of the Magistrates' Courts (Northern Ireland) Order 1981 (definition of " domestic proceedings " for the purposes of that Order), in paragraph (*a*), after " Part I of the Maintenance Orders (Reciprocal Enforcement) Act 1972 " insert " or under Part I of the Civil Jurisdiction and Judgments Act 1982 so far as that Part relates to the recognition and enforcement of maintenance orders ".

(2) In Article 98 of that Order (enforcement of orders for periodical payment of money), in sub-paragraph (*b*) of paragraph (11), after " Part I of the Maintenance Orders (Reciprocal Enforcement) Act 1972 " insert " or Part I of the Civil Jurisdiction and Judgments Act 1982 ".

SCH. 12

PART II

AMENDMENTS CONSEQUENTIAL ON SCHEDULE 8

Law Reform (Miscellaneous Provisions) (Scotland) Act 1940 (*c.* 42)

1. In the Law Reform (Miscellaneous Provisions) (Scotland) Act 1940 after section 4(2) there shall be inserted the following subsection—

"(3) This section does not apply—

(*a*) in the case of an agreement entered into after the dispute in respect of which the agreement is intended to have effect has arisen ; or

(*b*) where the contract is one referred to in Rule 3 of Schedule 8 to the Civil Jurisdiction and Judgments Act 1982.".

Maintenance Orders Act 1950 (*c.* 37)

2. In section 15(1)(*b*) of the Maintenance Orders Act 1950 for the words "for separation and aliment" there shall be substituted the words "which contains a conclusion for aliment not falling within the scope of paragraph (*a*)(i) above".

Maintenance Orders (Reciprocal Enforcement) Act 1972 (*c.* 18)

3.—(1) In section 4 of the Maintenance Orders (Reciprocal Enforcement) Act 1972 (power of the sheriff to make a provisional maintenance order against a person residing in a reciprocating country) the following subsection shall be substituted for subsections (1) and (2)—

"(1) In any action where the sheriff has jurisdiction by virtue of Rule 2(5) of Schedule 8 to the Civil Jurisdiction and Judgments Act 1982 and the defender resides in a reciprocating country, any maintenance order granted by the sheriff shall be a provisional order.".

(2) In subsections (3), (4) and (5) of that section for the words "in which the sheriff has jurisdiction by virtue of" there shall be substituted in each place where they occur the words "referred to in".

Consumer Credit Act 1974 (*c.* 39)

4. In section 141 of the Consumer Credit Act 1974 the following subsections shall be substituted for subsection (3)—

"(3) In Scotland the sheriff court shall have jurisdiction to hear and determine any action referred to in subsection (1) and such an action shall not be brought in any other court.

(3A) Subject to subsection (3B) an action which is brought in the sheriff court by virtue of subsection (3) shall be brought only in one of the following courts, namely—

(*a*) the court for the place where the debtor or hirer is domiciled (within the meaning of section 41 or 42 of the Civil Jurisdiction and Judgments Act 1982) ;

(*b*) the court for the place where the debtor or hirer carries on business ; and

(*c*) where the purpose of the action is to assert, declare or determine proprietary or possessory rights, or rights of security, in or over moveable property, or to obtain authority to dispose of moveable property, the court for the place where the property is situated.

(3B) Subsection (3A) shall not apply—

(*a*) where Rule 3 of Schedule 8 to the said Act of 1982 applies ; or

(*b*) where the jurisdiction of another court has been prorogated by an agreement entered into after the dispute has arisen.".

PART III

AMENDMENTS CONSEQUENTIAL ON SECTION 36

Maintenance Orders Act 1950 (*c*.37)

1.—(1) The Maintenance Orders Act 1950 is amended as follows.

(2) In section 18 (enforcement of registered orders), after subsection (3A) insert—

"(3B) Notwithstanding subsection (1) above, no court in Northern Ireland in which a maintenance order is registered under this Part of this Act shall enforce that order to the extent that it is for the time being registered in another court in Northern Ireland under section 36 of the Civil Jurisdiction and Judgments Act 1982.".

(3) In section 21(2) (evidence admissible before court where order registered)—

(*a*) in paragraph (*a*) after " 1958 " insert " or under section 36 of the Civil Jurisdiction and Judgments Act 1982 " ;

(*b*) after " that Act " (twice) insert " of 1958 " ;

(*c*) after paragraph (*b*) insert—

" (*c*) registered in a court in Northern Ireland under section 36 of the Civil Jurisdiction and Judgments Act 1982 ".

(4) In section 24(3) (notice of cancellation of order to be given to other courts interested), after " Part I of the Maintenance Orders Act 1958 " insert " or section 36 of the Civil Jurisdiction and Judgments Act 1982 ".

Maintenance Orders Act 1958 (*c*. 39)

2. In section 23(2) of the Maintenance Orders Act 1958 (provisions which extend to Scotland and Northern Ireland) after " section 2 " insert " section 2A ".

SCH. 12

Maintenance and Affiliation Orders Act (Northern Ireland) 1966 (*c.* 35) (*N.I.*)

3.—(1) The Maintenance and Affiliation Orders Act (Northern Ireland) 1966 is amended as follows.

(2) At the beginning of section 9 (introductory provisions relating to registration in one court of maintenance order made by another) insert " Without prejudice to section 36 of the Civil Jurisdiction and Judgments Act 1982,".

(3) In section 10 (orders to which Part II applies), after subsection (1) insert—

" (1A) This Part, except sections 11, 11A and 14(2) and (3), also applies in accordance with section 36 of the Civil Jurisdiction and Judgments Act 1982 to maintenance orders made by a court in England and Wales or Scotland and registered in Northern Ireland under Part II of the Maintenance Orders Act 1950.".

(4) In section 13 (variation of orders registered in courts of summary jurisdiction), after subsection (7) insert—

"(7A) No application for any variation in respect of a registered order shall be made to any court in respect of an order made by the High Court of Justice in England or the Court of Session and registered in that court under section 36 of the Civil Jurisdiction and Judgments Act 1982.

Judgments Enforcement (Northern Ireland) Order 1981 (*S.I.* 1981/266 (*N.I.* 6))

4. In Article 98 of the Judgments Enforcement (Northern Ireland) Order 1981, (powers of courts to make attachment of earnings orders), in sub-paragraph (iv) of paragraph (*a*) at the end add " but not subsequently registered in a court of summary jurisdiction under section 36 of the Civil Jurisdiction and Judgments Act 1982 ".

Magistrates' Courts (Northern Ireland) Order 1981 (*S.I.* 1981/1675 (*N.I.* 26))

5.—(1) In Article 88 of the Magistrates' Courts (Northern Ireland) Order 1981 (definition of " domestic proceedings " for the purposes of that Order)—

(*a*) in paragraph (*a*), delete the words " or the Maintenance Orders Act 1950 ";

(*b*) after paragraph (*a*) insert—

" (*aa*) in relation to maintenance orders registered in a court of summary jurisdiction under the Maintenance Orders Act 1950 or Part II of the Maintenance and Affiliation Orders Act (Northern Ireland) 1966 or section 36 of the Civil Jurisdiction and Judgments Act 1982, under that Act of 1950 or Part II of that Act of 1966 ".

(2) In Article 98 of that Order (enforcement of orders for periodical payment of money), in sub-paragraph (*d*) of paragraph (11), at the end add—

" or under section 36 of the Civil Jurisdiction and Judgments Act 1982 ".

SCHEDULE 13

Section 53.

COMMENCEMENT, TRANSITIONAL PROVISIONS AND SAVINGS

PART I

COMMENCEMENT

Provisions coming into force on Royal Assent

1. The following provisions come into force on Royal Assent:

Provision	*Subject-matter*
section 53(1) and Part I of this Schedule.	Commencement.
section 55	Short title.

Provisions coming into force six weeks after Royal Assent

2. The following provisions come into force at the end of the period of six weeks beginning with the day on which this Act is passed:

Provision	*Subject-matter*
section 24(1)(*a*), (2)(*a*) and (3).	Interim relief and protective measures in cases of doubtful jurisdiction.
section 29	Service of county court process outside Northern Ireland.
section 30	Proceedings in England and Wales or Northern Ireland for torts to immovable property.
section 31	Overseas judgments given against states.
section 32	Overseas judgments given in breach of agreement for settlement of disputes.
section 33	Certain steps not to amount to submission to jurisdiction of overseas court.
section 34	Certain judgments a bar to further proceedings on the same cause of action.
section 35(3)	Consolidation of Orders in Council under section 14 of the Administration of Justice Act 1920. (1920 c. 81.)
section 38	Overseas judgments counteracting an award of multiple damages.
section 40	Power to modify enactments relating to legal aid, etc.
section 49	Saving for powers to stay, sist, strike out or dismiss proceedings.
section 50	Interpretation: general.
section 51	Application to Crown.
section 52	Extent.

SCH. 13

Provision	*Subject-matter*
paragraphs 7 to 10 of Part II of this Schedule and section 53(2) so far as relates to those paragraphs.	Transitional provisions and savings.
section 54 and Schedule 14 so far as relating to the repeal of provisions in section 4 of the Foreign Judgments (Reciprocal Enforcement) Act 1933.	Repeals consequential on sections 32 and 33.

1933 c. 13.

Provisions coming into force on a day to be appointed

3.—(1) The other provisions of this Act come into force on such day as the Lord Chancellor and the Lord Advocate may appoint by order made by statutory instrument.

(2) Different days may be appointed under this paragraph for different purposes.

PART II

TRANSITIONAL PROVISIONS AND SAVINGS

Section 16 *and Schedule* 4

1.—(1) Section 16 and Schedule 4 shall not apply to any proceedings begun before the commencement of that section.

(2) Nothing in section 16 or Schedule 4 shall preclude the bringing of proceedings in any part of the United Kingdom in connection with a dispute concerning a contract if the parties to the dispute had agreed before the commencement of that section that the contract was to be governed by the law of that part of the United Kingdom.

Section 18 *and Schedule* 6 *and associated repeals*

2.—(1) In relation to a judgment a certificate whereof has been registered under the 1868 Act or the 1882 Act before the repeal of that Act by this Act, the 1868 Act or, as the case may be, the 1882 Act shall continue to have effect notwithstanding its repeal.

(2) Where by virtue of sub-paragraph (1) the 1882 Act continues to have effect in relation to an order to which section 47 of the Fair Employment (Northern Ireland) Act 1976 (damages etc. for unfair discrimination) applies, that section shall continue to have effect in relation to that order notwithstanding the repeal of that section by this Act.

1976 c. 25.

(3) A certificate issued under Schedule 6 shall not be registered under that Schedule in a part of the United Kingdom if the judgment to which that certificate relates is the subject of a certificate registered in that part under the 1868 Act or the 1882 Act.

(4) In this paragraph— SCH. 13

" the 1868 Act " means the Judgments Extension Act 1868 ; 1868 c. 54.

" the 1882 Act " means the Inferior Courts Judgments Extension Act 1882 ; 1882 c. 31.

" judgment " has the same meaning as in section 18.

Section 18 *and Schedule* 7

3. Schedule 7 and, so far as it relates to that Schedule, section 18 shall not apply to judgments given before the coming into force of that section.

Section 19

4. Section 19 shall not apply to judgments given before the commencement of that section.

Section 20 *and Schedule* 8

5. Section 20 and Schedule 8 shall not apply to any proceedings begun before the commencement of that section.

Section 26

6. The power conferred by section 26 shall not be exercisable in relation to property arrested before the commencement of that section or in relation to bail or other security given—

(*a*) before the commencement of that section to prevent the arrest of property ; or

(*b*) to obtain the release of property arrested before the commencement of that section ; or

(*c*) in substitution (whether directly or indirectly) for security given as mentioned in sub-paragraph (*a*) or (*b*).

Section 31

7. Section 31 shall not apply to any judgment—

(*a*) which has been registered under Part II of the Administration of Justice Act 1920 or Part I of the Foreign Judgments (Reciprocal Enforcement) Act 1933 before the time when that section comes into force ; or 1920 c. 81. 1933 c. 13.

(*b*) in respect of which proceedings at common law for its enforcement have been finally determined before that time.

Section 32 *and associated repeal*

8.—(1) Section 32 shall not apply to any judgment—

(*a*) which has been registered under Part II of the Administration of Justice Act 1920, Part I of the Foreign Judgments (Reciprocal Enforcement) Act 1933 or Part I of the Maintenance Orders (Reciprocal Enforcement) Act 1972 before the time when that section comes into force ; or 1972 c. 18.

(*b*) in respect of which proceedings at common law for its enforcement have been finally determined before that time.

SCH. 13

1933 c. 13. (2) Section 4(3)(*b*) of the Foreign Judgments (Reciprocal Enforcement) Act 1933 shall continue to have effect, notwithstanding its repeal by this Act, in relation to a judgment registered under Part I of that Act before the commencement of section 32.

Section 33 *and associated repeal*

9.—(1) Section 33 shall not apply to any judgment—

1920 c. 81. (*a*) which has been registered under Part II of the Administration of Justice Act 1920 or Part I of the Foreign Judgments (Reciprocal Enforcement) Act 1933 before the time when that section comes into force ; or

(*b*) in respect of which proceedings at common law for its enforcement have been finally determined before that time.

(2) The repeal by this Act of words in section 4(2)(*a*)(i) of the Foreign Judgments (Reciprocal Enforcement) Act 1933 shall not affect the operation of that provision in relation to a judgment registered under Part I of that Act before the commencement of section 33.

Section 34

10. Section 34 shall not apply to judgments given before the commencement of that section.

Section 54.

SCHEDULE 14

REPEALS

Chapter	Short title	Extent of repeal
41 Geo. 3. c. 90.	Crown Debts Act 1801.	The preamble. Sections 1 to 8.
5 Geo. 4. c. 111.	Crown Debts Act 1824.	The whole Act.
22 & 23 Vict. c. 21.	Queen's Remembrancer Act 1859.	Section 24.
31 & 32 Vict. c. 54.	Judgments Extension Act 1868.	The whole Act.
31 & 32 Vict. c. 96.	Ecclesiastical Buildings and Glebes (Scotland) Act 1868.	In section 4, the words " of the county in which the parish concerned is situated " and the words from " provided " to the end.
45 & 46 Vict. c. 31.	Inferior Courts Judgments Extension Act 1882.	The whole Act.
7 Edw. 7. c. 51.	Sheriff Courts (Scotland) Act 1907.	In section 5, the words from the first " Provided " to " that jurisdiction ".
14 & 15 Geo. 5. c. 27.	Conveyancing (Scotland) Act 1924.	In section 23(6) the words from " of the county " to " is situated ".

SCH. 14

Chapter	Short title	Extent of repeal
23 & 24 Geo. 5. c. 13.	Foreign Judgments (Reciprocal Enforcement) Act 1933.	In section 4(2)(*a*)(i), the words from " otherwise " to " that court ". Section 4(3)(*b*). In section 9(1), the word " superior " in both places where it occurs. In section 11(1), the definition of " Judgments given in the superior courts of the United Kingdom ". In section 12, in paragraph (*a*) the words from " (except " to " this Act) ", and paragraph (*d*). In section 13(*b*), the words " and section two hundred and thirteen ", " respectively " and " and 116 ".
14 Geo. 6. c. 37.	Maintenance Orders Act 1950.	Section 6. Section 8. Section 9(1)(*a*). In section 16(2)(*b*)(v), the words from the beginning to " or ".
4 & 5 Eliz. 2. c. 46.	Administration of Justice Act 1956.	Section 51(*a*).
1963 c. 22.	Sheriff Courts (Civil Jurisdiction and Procedure) (Scotland) Act 1963.	Section 3(2).
1965 c. 2.	Administration of Justice Act 1965.	In Schedule 1 the entry relating to the Crown Debts Act 1801.
1971 c. 55.	Law Reform (Jurisdiction in Delict) (Scotland) Act 1971.	The whole Act.
1972 c. 18.	Maintenance Orders (Reciprocal Enforcement) Act 1972.	In section 40— (*a*) in paragraph (*a*), the words " against persons in that country or territory "; and (*b*) in paragraph (*b*), the words " against persons in the United Kingdom ". In section 47(3), the words " or having ceased to reside ". In the Schedule, paragraph 4.
1976 c. 25.	Fair Employment (Northern Ireland) Act 1976.	Section 47.
1978 c. 23.	Judicature (Northern Ireland) Act 1978.	In Part II of Schedule 5— (*a*) the entry relating to the Crown Debts Act 1801; and (*b*) in the entry relating to the Foreign Judgments (Reciprocal Enforcement) Act 1933, the word " respectively ", where last occurring, and the words " and 116 ".

Sch. 14

Chapter	Short title	Extent of repeal
1981 c. 54	Supreme Court Act 1981.	In Schedule 5, paragraph 2 of the entry relating to the Foreign Judgments (Reciprocal Enforcement) Act 1933.

PRINTED IN ENGLAND BY PAUL FREEMAN
Controller and Chief Executive of Her Majesty's Stationery Office and
Queen's Printer of Acts of Parliament.

1ST IMPRESSION JULY 1982

5TH IMPRESSION DECEMBER 1993

Dd 5061787 12/93 C3 5160 61743 Ord 270190